Daddy's Little
Secret

Daddy's Little Secret

**Pregnant at fourteen and there's
only one man who can be the father**

TINA DAVIS

EBURY
PRESS

3 5 7 9 10 8 6 4

This edition published 2011
First published in 2011 by Ebury Press, an imprint of Ebury Publishing
A Random House Group company

The Random House Group Limited Reg. No. 954009

Addresses for companies within the Random House Group can be found at
www.randomhouse.co.uk

A CIP catalogue record for this book is available from the British Library

The Random House Group Limited supports the Forest Stewardship
Council® (FSC®), the leading international forest certification organisation.
All our titles that are printed on Greenpeace approved FSC® certified paper
carry the FSC® logo. Our paper procurement policy can be found at
www.randomhouse.co.uk/environment.

MIX
Paper from
responsible sources
FSC® C016897

Designed and set by seagulls.net

Printed and bound in the UK by CPI Cox & Wyman, Reading, RG1 8EX

ISBN 9780091941000

*'Every area of trouble gives out a ray of hope;
and the one unchangeable certainty is that
nothing is certain or unchangeable.'*

J F Kennedy

Contents

Prologue

I had never been on a train before, but I thought it was brilliant. Sitting by the window, I stared out open-mouthed at the houses as they whizzed past. My breath steamed up the window, but I quickly wiped the condensation away with my sleeve. Sitting in the carriage with my mum, two-year-old sister Lisa and baby brother Paul, I felt that I was heading towards an exciting new life.

All too soon, the train pulled into a train station. We collected our bags from where they had been stowed away. It was time to leave the carriage. But as I stood at the doorway, I couldn't move.

A big gap had opened up between the train and the platform and far below I could see the dark, dirty tracks. I was a small child, and I didn't think I'd be able to get across without falling into the crack.

That day I was wearing my favourite outfit – a pair of pink flowery culottes with a white shirt and matching pink collar. The top and shorts were connected with a pink scarf that tied with a bow at the front. I'd also worn my best shoes, which had blue lace bows and little black buttons. I loved those shoes.

'*What if I fell into the gap?*' I thought. '*I'd get my outfit all dirty, or lose a shoe. Or worse, I could die!*'

In my small chubby hands, I clutched my black wheelie bag for dear life and looked pleadingly up at Mum.

'I can't do it,' I whimpered, shaking my head, which made my pigtails flap against my cheeks.

'Come on, Tina,' she yelled as she struggled off the train with the pram, holding my baby brother Paul. Toddler Lisa had already made it on to the platform, and if she could, surely a big seven-year-old like me could too. So taking a deep breath I jumped – and landed safely on the other side, to my great relief.

Now we bundled down the platform with all our bags and suitcases – Mum pushing my brother, my younger sister Lisa on reins and me holding the side of the pram with one hand, and yanking my bag along with the other.

As we walked towards the barrier a man was there to greet us on the other side. He wore a pair of horrible cream trousers, a white shirt and brown shoes. He had thin blond hair in a quiff over a thin face and was grinning from ear to ear.

Mum's face lit up with eager anticipation and then she threw herself into his arms for a long embrace. When she finally let him go, she turned to us. 'Kids, this is Charlie.'

I nodded at the blond man and he leaned down to me, eyes wide and full of smiles.

'You must be the lovely Tina!' he said. 'What a sweet thing you are! I've got lots of lovely surprises for you.'

I didn't think much of it at the time; he was just another man. And there had already been so many men in Mum's life.

But if I'd known the destruction and terror Charlie would bring to my world, I would have turned and jumped back on that train, however big the gap.

Chapter 1

Mum

Life at home had always been difficult and chaotic with Mum. I found out much later on that she'd suffered from paranoid schizophrenia, but as a kid all I knew was there were two sides to her.

There was the lovely, bubbly woman who could make everyone smile and laugh, and then there was the horrible woman who hit me, shouted at me and said hateful, hurtful things.

From the word go, I was made to feel like an inconvenience in her life.

Every day she'd tell me, 'I hate you! You were a mistake,' and crushingly, 'I wish you'd never been born.'

She never made me feel as if I was wanted or loved. Is it any wonder, then, that I grew up thinking that I was unlovable?

As a baby I was in hospital a lot, mainly for bladder infections, but once my mum smacked my head against a door and another time I was pushed down a flight of stairs in my pram. I found out from my social services' files that both times my granddad had reported Mum to the authorities but nothing ever came of it.

Despite it all, I did love her. She was my mum but she wasn't very nice to me.

My earliest memory is of my mum telling me that everybody dies someday. I was playing with my dolly on her bed, my legs swinging over the sides, when Mum sat down next to me, clearly upset.

She put her arm around me and leaned against me. I leaned back. It was so rare that my mum showed me any affection, that whenever she did I was so grateful to her.

'The thing you have to realise, Tina, is that people die,' she said simply. 'That's a fact of life. One day you're here and the next day you're gone. It's going to happen to me, to you, to all of us.'

I don't know what made her want to tell a three-year-old that people die, that she was going to die, and that I would too. It frightened me and I didn't under-stand what she was trying to say. In my confused little mind, I thought she was telling me that she was going to pass away soon, so I started to cry.

At first Mum and my dad Tony were happy together. We lived in a small flat just outside a big town in the Midlands. Dad was a driver and sometimes Mum used to take me down to the yard to see him when he was on his dinner break. He was short, with a big chest and a shaved head. I liked Dad back then. He decorated my bedroom with Danger Mouse wallpaper and he used to take me fishing down the canal. Once I caught an eel, but when it came up it was all wrapped up round my pole and wriggling like mad so I ran off screaming.

But soon the arguments started. I'd sit upstairs in my bedroom, listening as Dad interrogated Mum about where she'd been. Mum had some friends who lived at the bottom of our road, the kind of people who liked to party all the time. She'd be out half the night with them, leaving Dad and me alone at home.

When she got back, Dad would start on her. 'Where have you been Susan?' he'd roar. 'What have you been up to?'

Mum wasn't a very good liar. She always got caught out, saying she'd been out with a friend, but then Dad would say he'd seen that same friend and she wasn't with her. The fact was Mum was always out seeing other fellas. After a bit of yelling, she'd storm out and we wouldn't see her for a couple of days. My grandparents – Mum's parents – would look after me while Dad was at work, then Mum would come back and she and Dad would have yet another row. That quickly became our routine.

My sister Lisa was born when I was five and my brother Paul came along two years after her. Of course, Mum told Dad they were his. We found out much later from Mum that he wasn't their dad, so they were only my half-brother and -sister; but Dad believed they were his and his name went on their birth certificates.

Mum could be lively and funny, especially when we went round to see her sister, Tanya. She'd bundle me up, put Lisa in her pram, and walk the short distance to Auntie Tanya's house.

They'd reminisce about when they were younger together and I'd watch them crease up with laughter at their girlish adventures on the estate where they grew up.

Tanya had a little girl called Carly and we used to play together, jumping on the beds or running round the house singing. Later, if our mums were feeling energetic, they'd chase us round and round the house until we all collapsed laughing in a big heap in the living room. They were good times and I always looked forward to staying at Tanya's place. There was no tension there, unlike at my house where Mum and Dad were always arguing. And Carly's mum doted on her, unlike mine. Her room was crowded with toys and games, whereas I only really had my dolly to play with. And going round to Tanya's meant that I had someone to have fun with – usually at home I was ignored or I crept around trying not to upset anyone, so it was lovely to have somewhere to go where I felt welcomed.

Sometimes, we'd go down to my nana and granddad's house a mile and a half away from our home. I loved it there. They had all these videos we could watch and two little dogs named Bella and Meg, but we called them 'The Ankle Biters'. Nana and Granddad cuddled me, they bought me things like toys and sweets, and whenever Granddad came in from work he'd call from the front door, 'Where's my Tiny Tina?' It was his special name for me and after he'd come in and sat down, I'd crawl in on all fours, pretending to be cat and start purring and meowing. Then, he'd sit me on his knee and ask me about my day. I was happy at their house and I felt loved.

At home it was a different story. For some reason, my own mother just didn't want to be around me. She hated me. And she made sure I knew it. Every day I heard the same spiteful words, telling me I wasn't loved. I tried to ignore it – after all, she was my mum. Out in public she was okay – she treated me like her daughter and didn't put me down in front of other people, but on our own, she'd change. She didn't want to know, I became a total nobody. If I asked her a question, she'd ignore me. She always seemed to have something more important to do than talk to me.

I remember going to my room quite a lot crying but she never once came up to comfort me. I'd just be left there.

When Dad came in, Mum would tell him: 'She's been naughty, leave her.' So he wouldn't come up to see me. It was her way of making sure that nobody was nice to me.

She barely ever touched me, let alone cuddled or hugged me. I can't remember her once saying she loved me. Not once.

But back then, I believed she loved me because she was my mum and mothers are supposed to love their children, aren't they? As a child you can't think any different.

So any small gesture, I took to be a sign of affection. If she was talking to me normally, not being nasty or saying hurtful things, I thought that meant she loved me. That way I could believe that she did care about me. After all, she wasn't mean to my brother and sister. She loved them to bits.

Over time, the fights between my parents got even worse and Mum took us with her when she stormed out. We'd go and stay at our auntie Tanya's or at Nana's or at Mum's friends' houses. And then Mum started taking us round to houses of men we didn't know.

These were fellas Mum had met through chat lines. Sometimes when she and Dad had had a fight, we'd end up staying at these strangers' houses for weeks on end. After a while we might move to another bloke's house, then we might go back to Tanya's and eventually we'd land back at home again.

I just did as I was told. If Mum said, 'Come on, pack your bag, we're leaving', I packed my bag and left with her.

She didn't always take me with her though. One time, during a brief period when Mum and Dad were back together, we were staying with their friends Myra and Harry as our house had been broken into. They were really nice people and had a girl and a boy, Katie and Simon, so we used to play together. They lived on the third floor of a block of flats and I shared a room with Katie, which overlooked an alleyway that went under the flats. My sister was nearly two and Paul was just a baby.

We'd been there nearly four months when an argument broke out between Mum and Dad. She'd gone out and when Dad asked her where she'd been she'd lied and said she was with a girlfriend. But someone saw her with this other guy and he came round to Myra and Harry's to confront her about it.

Us kids were sent upstairs and locked in the bedroom. My sister sat on the bed playing with some toys while me and Katie listened to the shouting downstairs.

'How could you do this to me, you bitch?' I heard Dad shout.

Harry was trying to calm my dad down because he was getting really angry and Myra was shouting at my mum. I was crying.

The next minute we heard doors banging. I looked out of the bedroom window to see my mum walking away down the alleyway with Paul in his pram. She knew that Lisa and I were in that bedroom but not once did she turn round and look at me. She just walked away as if she didn't have a care in the world. And she took my brother with her.

Later on that evening, I had to go to the toilet so I was banging on the door to be let out. Dad thumped up the stairs, opened the door, grabbed hold of me and threw me into the bathroom, bruising my arm down the side. And when I'd finished he threw me back into the bedroom and locked the door again.

'Why are they locking me in?' I worried. *'Have I been naughty?'*

I was seven and it scared me. It scared the hell out of me.

We must have been there for a week without Mum. Every night I'd sit at the window, crying, waiting for her to walk back down the alleyway, hoping that she'd come back. Every footstep I heard I wanted to be hers. But it never was

Then Dad was so miserable and would get tetchy with me and Lisa – even when we were good. I didn't know what was going on, all I knew was that I just wanted Mum to come back.

And then she did. I was walking back from the shops with Dad one day; Lisa was in the house with Myra and Harry. Suddenly, a police car pulled up next to us and a policeman got out. He grabbed hold of my hand, took me off my dad and bundled me into the back of the police car. I didn't know what was going on and started crying. Then the policeman went into the house with Dad and took my sister out. Then, he put her in the back of a police car and drove off. We were later reunited with my mum. It turned out that she'd gone to the police and told them that our father had run off, taking me and my sister with him, leaving her alone with the baby. Lies, of course they were, but she was able to convince the police that Lisa and I had been taken away by my father. She told them other lies too; a policeman told me that my dad was violent and he would hit me and shout at me all the time.

The funny thing is, apart from that one incident when he was upset, I don't remember Dad being violent. Mum made a lot of that stuff up, or at least exaggerated the situation. The problem was there was no one saying anything different so after a while I started to believe her.

'He always used to push you around, Tina. Don't you remember?' Mum would prompt. Then, she'd describe the event in great detail. It seemed so real when she was talking about it that I believed it had happened.

It got to the point where I became terrified of my dad because I believed he did all these awful things, even though I had no real memory of them. But when you're a kid and you've only got your mum telling you one story, you don't question it.

Once again, we were on the move. Mum could never stick anywhere for long and we moved from one place to another, sometimes to fellas' houses, sometimes to hotels and once to a caravan. The longest time we stayed anywhere was when we went to live with Auntie Tanya for three months and Mum even put me into the school near her house, but soon we were packing our bags again.

I never understood why we kept moving. There was never any discussion or explanation. Mum would get the bags out and announce, 'Come on, we're leaving.' And that would be that.

When we went to different guys' places she'd just say 'This is Rob' or 'This is Mark'. And then we'd live with them for a bit. I accepted it because I didn't have any choice and it quickly became the normal state of affairs. I was constantly changing schools, but it never fazed me. I just accepted that was the way things were.

Sometimes in the middle of the day Mum would go off to the bedroom with whoever we were staying with but it didn't bother me. I'd sit in the living room watching my favourite cartoons like *Dogtanian*, *Mr Benn* or *The Moomins* while Lisa played nearby and Paul slept in his cot.

I now know what they were doing, but when you're seven, cartoons are the most important thing in your life and adult stuff doesn't really interest you.

One man we stayed with was a security guard at a supermarket. He was nice and friendly and he had a record player, which was brilliant. I used to love putting on records and dancing around the room, holding a hairbrush for a microphone. My favourite was 'Toy Boy' by Sinitta and I listened to it over and over again.

After the hundredth time of playing it, the record started to jump – I'd scratched it! I was scared in case Mum's boyfriend found out, so I hid the record down the side of the cabinet. But three days later, he was off work for the weekend and was going through his albums when he discovered the ruined record.

'What have you done?' he raged, after trying to listen to it.

'It wasn't me!' I lied. I didn't want to get into trouble or make Mum mad at me too.

But he knew better. 'You're the only one who listens to it! You were obsessed with it. Now I know why you haven't played it for days,' he fumed. 'You broke it, you silly little girl. Just admit it and stop lying to me!'

I looked over at Mum, who was filing her nails on the settee, but she just raised her eyebrows as if to say, 'Well?'

Mum never stuck up for me. Here was a complete stranger having a go at her kid but she never once said anything to him.

The security guard would get up in the morning and go to work and Mum would get on the phone and then sit on the chat lines all day. She must have run up a fortune in calls on this guy's bill. And most often, I heard her talking to someone called Charlie.

Three days after the record incident, we were packing our bags again.

When we'd left wherever we'd been staying at before, we'd always go on to the next place on the bus or in a car, but this time we got on a train. It was so exciting – I'd never been on a train before and I loved the way we moved so fast. I loved seeing the world rushing by, and I loved watching the other passengers reading the papers or sipping the cup of tea they had bought from the trolley that rattled its way down the aisle of the carriage. It was all so new to me and different – could it be that we were going on to a brand-new and exciting life? Were things finally going to change?

I didn't want the trip to end but when we pulled into a station, Mum told us all to get off and that's when we were introduced to Charlie.

My heart sank. We were going to stay with yet another stranger. I knew straight away it was the man she'd been talking to on the phone but I didn't say anything.

Charlie put his arm around my mum and gave her a cuddle. Then he picked up our bags and led us out to the taxi to take us back to his place.

I didn't think anything of it then. He was just another man. I guess I thought we wouldn't be there long.

Chapter 2
Charlie

When we arrived at Charlie's home, I was pleased to see it was a nice place, not scruffy like some of the houses Mum had taken us to. It was a terraced house on a neat, tree-lined street, and although it wasn't a particularly posh area, the houses were all well maintained. Perhaps it wouldn't be so bad living here after all.

There were brown–green carpets all through the house and in the living room there was a settee, two chairs and a TV. At the back there was a tiny enclosed patio garden with a back gate leading to the alley. Lisa and I even had our own room upstairs. But best of all, there were toys and books! It was great – none of Mum's other men had ever bought us stuff.

Charlie seemed happy Mum had come and genuinely pleased to have us kids there too. He made a real effort to be nice to me. I didn't think much of it at first. After all, he was just another bloke, this was just another house. I was waiting for the moment when I'd come home and Mum would have all the bags packed. But it never happened and in time Charlie won me over.

On my eighth birthday, he bought me a cake and we went round to his auntie Pam's house for a little party where we all watched *Annie*, the musical about a little orphan girl who gets adopted by a millionaire. I loved it, especially the songs 'Hard Knock Life' and 'Tomorrow'. I sat, rapt, avidly watching every frame, right until the end when Annie's name was spelled out in the fireworks display that Daddy Warbucks put on for her. I loved it.

After the video was over, Charlie beckoned me outside, promising a great big surprise and when I came out, I was amazed to see a beautiful pink and white bike leaning against the side of the house. Oh my God, it was gorgeous – so shiny and new.

'Come on,' he said. 'Let's give it a go!'

I'd never ridden a bike before so I was scared, but it had stabilisers and Charlie took me to a deserted car park where I whizzed round and round, my hair streaming behind in the breeze, feeling carefree and happy for the first time in ages!

Over the next few weeks, I took my bike out every day and one Sunday Charlie said he would teach me how to ride it without stabilisers. I was thrilled, but nervous of course.

'Don't worry,' he yelled, holding onto the back of the bike. 'Just keep peddling. That's right – keep peddling. Keep going, keep going…faster!'

And when I looked back over my shoulder I saw he was some way in the distance and I was riding on my own without stabilisers!

I wobbled unsteadily for a couple more feet then toppled off and scraped my hands and knees, but it only took a few more tries before I was riding round on my own, just like a big girl.

After a while I forgot about moving and started to enjoy the fact that someone was being nice to me. For the first time I felt like I was wanted and loved. My mum hadn't changed her attitude towards me, it was Charlie who was giving me the attention I so desperately craved.

I went to the local primary school and even that was good. Before then, we'd moved around so much I was always the new girl, the outsider and got bullied a lot. But at this school I didn't get picked on or called names.

And at home we now had a pet, a big fat tortoise-shell cat called Tilly. We'd never had a pet in any of the places we'd lived before but Charlie loved animals. He showed me how to tickle her under the chin so she'd purr loudly or scratch behind her ears, which made her arch her back.

Tilly was a myriad of colours – brown, black, white and orange – and I loved curling up with her in front of the TV and stroking her soft fur, marvelling at all the different colours swirling together.

Mum wasn't keen though – she thought pets were dirty and whenever she came in and Tilly was on the settee, she'd knock her on the floor.

Mum didn't seem to like anything that made me happy. So as time went on and my naturally bubbly and out-going personality started to shine through, she got nastier.

She didn't like the fact that somebody was paying attention to me. On the Christmas after my eighth birthday, she was especially cruel. We were arguing and then she ordered me to take some clothes upstairs.

'No, I don't want to,' I sulked.

'You bloody well will, you stupid little bitch!' she screamed at the top of her voice. 'You'll do as I say or so help me…'

At that moment Charlie walked in.

'Leave her alone, Susan!' he shouted at her.

I stood there, mouth agape. I couldn't believe it – someone was actually sticking up for me!

But Mum wouldn't be told.

'NO! She's my kid and I'll talk to her any way I like!'

They started arguing over me right there and I felt the tears bubbling up inside me. This wasn't how it was meant to be. A mother should protect and look after her children, but I never felt that security with my mum. She was so unpredictable that I never knew what she was going to do next. And so I was barely prepared when Mum took one look at me, picked up the Yellow Pages and hurled it at my head. I ducked down and it missed me by a whisker.

Then she leapt out of her chair, grabbed me by the hair, pulled me up the stairs and threw me into my bedroom. There was hair everywhere and my head was bleeding. She took a big chunk out of my head and for months afterwards I couldn't put my hair up in a ponytail.

Mum hated the fact that Charlie was nice to me – and it was just me he was particularly nice to, not Lisa or Paul, which made me feel really special. He worked as a plumber so he had a bit of money to spend and whenever he had a few quid he'd buy me things – sweets, clothes, toys, whatever I wanted.

One time he came home with a pair of pink Barbie roller skates. They were the best things ever – I actually couldn't believe someone had bought me something so wonderful. Whenever Charlie took me to the shops, I'd put them on and he'd pull me along so I wouldn't fall.

Mum didn't like that – she always complained if I had my skates on.

'Why did you have to bring those stupid things out?' she demanded.

'I have to practise!' I said.

'Oh, leave her alone,' Charlie told her and inside I'd be smiling. Charlie was always on my side.

After a few months, I was good enough to go skating on my own and my friend Sam and I would fly down the path of a big hill near my house. But I hadn't yet learned to use the stoppers so I'd brake by skating onto the grass.

One day, I was going down the hill and tried to turn onto the grass, but instead I headed straight towards a big concrete lamppost with big metal rings on it.

'Owwww!' I yelled as I hit the post head on. I limped back home with a big, bruised eye.

Charlie ran straight to the bathroom to get some cotton wool and TCP then we sat on the settee as he bathed my eye.

'Just leave her, will you?' Mum snapped at him. 'Stop fussing. She'll be fine.'

But Charlie just ignored her and after five minutes Mum got up off the couch and stormed out of the living room. Charlie and I looked at each other and we both giggled.

'Hey there, Pumpkin,' Charlie smiled, putting his head round my door one morning after a particularly vicious outburst from Mum.

I was lying on the bed, curled up into a ball, big sobs racking my little body.

'What's up today?' he came over and sat down on the bed next to me, rubbing my back as I let all the tears flow.

'She…she hates me!' I wailed, my small voice thick with emotion.

'Oh, come here,' Charlie soothed, putting his arms out and I crawled into them, instantly feeling better for a hug. 'Your mum doesn't hate you, she's just in a bad mood today. And I don't hate you. I love you, so that's okay, isn't it?'

I looked up into his warm, smiling eyes, nodded, then wiped my snotty nose on the back of my arm.

'That's better,' he laughed. 'I think we should go downstairs and get a Wagon Wheel. What do you think?'

I nodded again. Charlie was always there for me and after a while I started to think of him as my dad. He was the only person in my life who was there for me, cared for me, stuck up for me and bought me things. That's what parents do – but until that moment I'd never had a parent who was so nice to me. Mum was horrible and my real dad Tony had never paid me much attention. Charlie was more of a role model than anyone else had been in my life.

In time I came to realise that Mum was never going to be nice to me so I gave up trying to get her to love me. And gradually, my feelings for her died too. If she wasn't going to love me, why should I love her? So I started to hate her back. And I became ashamed of her.

By now she'd put on a lot of weight and she didn't dress nicely. She was fat with short black hair and wore bright red lipstick, which didn't make her look sexy, as she thought, just strange. If you saw her in the street, she wouldn't be the kind of person you'd be proud to call your mum. But I was proud to call Charlie my dad and I was happy in my new home.

Unfortunately, we didn't stay there long – I didn't know this at the time but Mum hadn't kept in touch with my real dad. In fact, she'd been hiding from him. But somehow he managed to track us down and one day I came home from school to find the suitcases packed and loaded into Charlie's car. My heart sank – '*Oh no, here we go again!*' When I realised Charlie was actually coming with us, I felt slightly happier. But it was such a rushed and chaotic departure, Mum said we didn't have time to find Tilly.

'We'll just have to leave her behind,' she declared, opening the car door for me.

'No!' I whimpered. 'We can't leave Tilly – I love her!'

'Yeah? Well, tough! Just get in the car, will you?'

'Who's going to look after her?' I wailed from the back seat.

'Oh, shut up!' Mum snapped at me. 'The cat will be fine. Now stop your bloody snivelling.'

Next thing I knew we were living across town in a hotel. I missed Tilly but the hotel was fun. We had a big room in the back, which I loved because the room was partly underground. It meant the windows were high up so Lisa and I used to jump on the furniture and swing from the window ledge. Paul was too young to join in, but he seemed content.

One day there was a knock at the door. Charlie wasn't in so Mum went to see who it was. Suddenly she whispered to us, 'Hide on the floor!'

So we all got on the floor under the windowsill and I heard my real dad's voice.

'So, you thought I wouldn't find you?' he said.

'What are you doing here?' Mum hissed, then she closed the door behind her as she went out to speak to him.

By this time I was nine, and I hadn't seen my dad in nearly two years. After he tracked us down we were made to go and meet him in a contact centre. I didn't want to go – after all the bad things Mum had told me about him, I hated him.

At the centre, there was Mum and Charlie on a settee on one side of the room and Tony – it didn't feel right to call him 'Dad' anymore – and his girlfriend seated opposite them while Lisa and I played with Lego bricks on a table in the middle.

Tony came over and sat between Lisa and me then he started building the bricks into a tower and asking how we were.

'Fine,' I said in a small voice.

'What have you been up to?' he tried again.

'Nothing,' I replied. I stopped playing with the bricks then and turned my attention to a jigsaw puzzle.

I didn't want to know him. It was just after my ninth birthday and that day, when he left he handed me two birthday cards – one from him and the other from his parents, Nana and Granddad.

When I left I was so upset and angry I ripped them up and threw them over the fence in the car park. After all this time, I couldn't believe he really loved me.

A few weeks later Tony came to see us at the hotel. Lisa and I were both in the bedroom and I remember him coming into the room and sitting on the bed next to us.

'I'm really sorry, girls,' he started. 'I'm sorry for everything. I really love you both very much.'

Lisa and I looked at each other – we didn't know what the hell was going on!

Then he said, 'The fact is, kids, I have to say good-bye now. I won't be seeing you again.'

After he left I was angry and upset. Why didn't my own dad want to see us again? Didn't he love us? What about Nana and Granddad? Why didn't they want to see us? My childish mind didn't think there might be another reason, like Mum telling him he couldn't see us.

I had so many questions and no answers. Nobody would talk to me. I wanted to ask Mum but getting anything out of her was impossible. Most days she barely acknowledged my existence and if she did, it was usually to let me know that I was a mistake.

Years later I found out my real dad did try and write to us. Social services passed on letters but my mum threw them away. She didn't want him having anything to do with us. For her, he wasn't part of our new life – we had Charlie now.

Soon after my real dad walked out of our lives, Mum announced that she was taking me out shopping.

'We have to get you a dress,' she said.

'For what?' I quizzed.

'For the wedding, of course.'

We went to Tammy Girl and I picked out a lovely blue skirt with a matching blue waistcoat, white top and glittery blue shoes with silver buckles.

Twirling in front of the mirror, I felt like a princess in my swishy skirt and sparkly shoes.

I was pleased Mum and Charlie were getting married so that I could wear my nice outfit – and Charlie would be my proper daddy now so he would always look after me! I was thrilled that I'd be changing my name from Tina Davis to Tina Jenkins – a new last name, the same as my new father's, would mean the start of a new life.

Not that marriage improved his dress sense. On the day, he wore a horrible dark green suit. It was so revolting I could have puked! But Mum wore a nice blue dress, my brother Paul was in a black and white pageboy outfit and Lisa wore the same as me.

There weren't that many people there – just Charlie and his mum Carol, my nana and granddad and Auntie Paula. Mum had four sisters and one brother but for some reason no one else from the family came.

Charlie and Mum were married at a Register Office then we all went to the pub afterwards for the reception.

'Come and sit next to me,' Charlie insisted as we sat down for our meal. It seemed strange – surely he should be sitting next to my mum on their wedding day?

Then he started telling me how pretty I looked. He was sitting too close to me, invading my personal space, but I couldn't tell him how uncomfortable he was making me feel – I owed him too much, for the clothes he bought me, the attention he paid me and the way he made me feel special.

'Don't you look lovely today,' he whispered close to my ear. I could feel his stubbly chin brushing against my soft cheek. 'So nice and pretty in your little blue dress.'

I didn't know why but it made me feel awkward – why was he paying me all these compliments? It was creepy. It wasn't what he said, it was how he said it – silky and smoothly, in a flirtatious manner that I had only seen before on TV. I also felt strange because of the way he was looking at me, studying me too hard, looking as if he wanted to eat me up.

My cheeks coloured as I stared down at my blue shoes, dangling over the edge of my chair. He gave me a cuddle, then I looked up and caught my mum's eye. She was staring at Charlie and me. I gave her a big smile but she didn't smile back.

She saw the two of us together and she just turned away.

Chapter 3
Growing Up

Everything changed for me after Charlie and Mum got married.

Shortly after the wedding Mum got pregnant with my little brother Daniel, but the doctors found an ovarian tumour. The baby was growing at the same time as the tumour so they couldn't give her any treatment while she was pregnant. It didn't bother me much that Mum wasn't well but I hoped the baby would be okay.

She was in and out of hospital so that she could be monitored by the doctors and nurses there, and when she was away, us kids were left at home with Charlie.

That's when things got even creepier.

One night he said to me, 'Do you want to sleep in my bed tonight and watch TV?'

It was a treat to be able to stay up late so I went upstairs and fell asleep in his bed.

The next morning I woke up, rubbed my eyes and realised I was still in Charlie's bed. There he was, his big chest heaving up and down as loud snores filled the room. I didn't understand why he hadn't taken me into my own room when he went to bed instead of sleeping right next to me. It felt odd, waking up in my mum and dad's room but I didn't mind and I was too naïve to think much of it – I just rolled off the side of the bed and padded downstairs to make some toast.

When Mum was a few months pregnant we all moved again. This time to a three-bedroom house, which was not far from the local hospital. Charlie, or Dad as I now started calling him, had converted a small cupboard downstairs into a box room for me – I think he thought I'd find it cute but I didn't. I was scared because there were spiders in there.

All I could see when I was in bed was the light reflecting off the cobwebs and I kept imagining the spiders coming down onto my face while I was asleep.

One night I got so freaked out by the spiders I ran upstairs to Mum and Dad's room – their door was wide open and I stood there, transfixed in horror as I saw Mum naked on top of Dad, moving up and down.

Her back was to me as their bed was against the wall facing the door so she didn't see me standing there but Dad could see me.

And he just lay there, looking at me. It was a strange look – even worse than the spiders – so I shot out of there and back downstairs.

As a child, I didn't know what that look meant. But looking back, I know exactly what it was. It was a leer.

*

Once Daniel was born Mum was in hospital a lot for chemotherapy and I had to grow up fast to help Dad look after the other kids and the house.

My role in the family changed – now I wasn't just a kid, I was more like a mother, bathing, feeding and dressing the younger ones.

By this time we'd moved again, to a house a mile away where I had a nice room upstairs, facing the bathroom.

When Mum was back from hospital she'd be drugged up on painkillers, sleeping. And she lost all her hair. Dad moved his bed downstairs because he said it wasn't nice sleeping next to Mum any more and even told me that she wet the bed.

In the evenings, we'd sit watching the space show *V* or *The A-Team* and Dad always wanted me to sit next to him for a cuddle. I'd clamber up onto his lap and snuggle into his arms while he wrapped a big arm round my shoulders and sometimes stroked my long brown hair.

He was my dad, and I loved him. And it was nice.

But all that was about to change.

One night I was upstairs in my bedroom watching my bedside telly when Dad walked in. I thought he was going to tell me to turn off the TV as it was quite late but instead he sat on the side of the bed and in a strange, hard voice I'd not heard before he ordered, 'Pull up your nightie.'

I was startled and bewildered – what was going on? I didn't understand what was happening but he was my dad, so I did as I was told. He stared at me for a while as fear grew in my belly. This didn't feel right.

Then he unbuttoned his trousers and climbed on top of me. The next thing I felt was an unbelievable shooting pain as he put himself inside me.

'Oh my God!' I thought I was going to split into two. It was like he'd shoved a red-hot poker inside me and the knife-like agony just seemed to go on and on.

Then I started to cry. *'What was happening? When would it end?'*

'Don't scream,' he whispered angrily. 'Don't say nothing or you'll wake your mum up and she'll go mad at you.'

I just lay there in shock, hardly breathing from the pain and the weight of his huge body on top of me. I tried to focus on the raised, circular patterns of Artex on the walls.

Finally, after what felt like forever, he got off me.

'Pull your nightie back down,' he barked. And I did.

Then he pulled up his pants, sat on the edge of the bed again and spoke to me very slowly and quietly, making sure I could hear every word. 'If you tell anybody I'll kill you. And anyway, your mum wouldn't believe you and she wouldn't want to know you. And everyone will blame you because it's all your fault.'

Then he calmly walked out. I slowly pulled myself up from the bed, still in agony, and limped to the bathroom, sobbing.

I must have spent an hour in there, trying to clean myself. I felt so dirty, but no matter how much soap I used I couldn't get clean. I felt sick, sore and confused.

I was nine – I had no idea what had just happened, or why. I must have done something wrong, like Dad had said, it must have been my fault.

I remember not sleeping much that night. I just lay awake, staring at the ceiling, wondering what I'd done wrong to make Dad do that horrible thing to me. I had tried to be a good girl but maybe I'd done something bad without realising.

I did finally fall asleep though. For when I woke up the next morning and got out of bed I was surprised and confused when Dad greeted me on the landing with a big smile and the offer of a piece of toast.

'No thanks,' I said hurriedly then scampered downstairs. *'What was going on?'*

He was totally normal with me, but I was still sore from the night before, and looking at him made me feel dirty and upset.

For the next few days, I could barely look at him – every time I saw him, it brought back the memory of what he'd done and I felt sick.

I suppose that first time I'd hoped it would just be the once – sadly it was only the beginning of a new phase in my life. A new, horrendous reality I just had to get used to.

Dad would come into my bedroom around three or four times a week – always when Mum was asleep – and rape me. I became petrified of going to bed and once there, I barely slept. Every footstep I heard I thought was his. Sometimes he came in when I was already asleep – then he'd wake me up, sit on my bed and tell me what to do. Over time, he started wanting different things – he wanted me to touch him or play with him. Afterwards he'd get on top of me and have sex with me. I'd just stare at the patterns on the wall. That and imagining I was somewhere far, far away were the only things that would block out the pain. If I was concentrating on something else, it was like it wasn't happening to me.

When he'd finished he'd always say the same thing: if I told anybody he'd kill me, everybody would hate me and they wouldn't believe me anyway. Besides, it was my fault. The look in his eye made me believe his every word.

My nights became a living hell while my days weren't much better. Mum still picked on me and Dad acted like nothing was wrong the rest of the time – he still wanted me to sit next to him at night, but now I couldn't go near him. I was scared of him, scared of what he'd do to me.

Whenever he was near, I felt sick with worry – what was going to happen next? What was he going to do? My only relief was in the bathroom where I'd wash myself down for hours – I'd fill up the sink with soap and water and clean myself all over as well as down below.

I couldn't stop but no matter how much I washed and wiped myself, I could still smell him on me. I just couldn't seem to wash the scent of him away.

At school, I became a totally different person. Before, I'd been a very bubbly, lively little girl, running around the playground playing Kiss Chase, chatting to everybody, dancing and singing.

But after Dad started coming into my room at night I didn't want to talk to the other children and I didn't feel like playing silly playground games either – instead I'd take myself off to the top of the field at the end of the school grounds during break times and sit there on my own.

'*Do other dads do this?*' I wondered as the other kids ran around, laughing. '*How could they laugh if this happened to them? It must just be me – there's something bad about me.*'

Soon, the other kids picked up on how I'd stopped speaking to everyone and that's when the bullying started. They thought I was strange.

Nicola, a girl who I'd once been friends with, started it. She called me 'smelly' and 'fatty' and when I didn't answer back, the other kids picked it up and yelled it at me whenever I was in the playground on my own.

Whenever I walked past in the corridor they'd spit on the floor and called me 'disgusting'. Then, when the teacher's back was turned they'd use their rulers to flick paper and rubbers at me. I felt like I deserved it – after all, I was disgusting.

I used to sit and daydream. I'd imagine living in a perfect house with perfect parents and being really happy. They would treat me so well and I'd play all the time and nobody would shout at me or do horrible things to me in the night. I'd imagine that somewhere out there my real parents, the nice ones, were looking for me and one day they'd come and take me away and we'd all live happily ever after.

For a short while I could dream of a better life. And then I'd be brought back to reality with a bang or a slap or a visit to my bedroom.

It was hopeless – I wasn't even old enough to go to senior school but I already hated my life. I didn't want it any more. I didn't want to live.

I stopped thinking of Charlie as my dad – it didn't seem right that my dad would do this to me so in my mind he became Charlie again, although I continued to call him 'Dad' to his face.

I wanted to tell Mum what was happening, but I was terrified that she'd blame me.

After all, she never stopped reminding me how much she hated me and how I was a big mistake so why would she be there for me now?

For some reason, the rest of the family had stopped coming to see us and we didn't go round to Auntie Tanya's or my nana and granddad's house any more.

The only person who I had loved and trusted in the world was Charlie – and he was the very person who was turning my life into a nightmare.

I was trapped.

By now the abuse was constant and it wasn't confined to the bedroom.

One time I was in the bath and Charlie came into the bathroom.

'Let me wash your hair,' he said gruffly.

So I sat there, soaking wet as he lathered up my hair then washed off the soap.

'Right, get out of the bath,' he ordered.

I dreaded what was about to come next. Charlie closed the bathroom door, pulled his pants down then sat on the toilet. Then he put me on top of him and had sex with me.

After he was finished he just picked me up and put me back in the bath. Then he walked out like nothing had happened. Sick to my stomach, I sat in that bath scrubbing and scrubbing until my skin was red and stinging. It felt so wrong but I didn't know how to stop it.

Around that time, I made a friend. Her name was Emma and she lived across the road from me. We also went to the same school, but because of the bullies who thought I was deeply uncool Emma didn't feel comfortable speaking to me there. So it was only went we went to Brownies once a week that Emma and I would play together. That was fun – at Brownies I could forget about home, forget about Charlie and just be a kid again.

Charlie didn't like it of course – he'd now become very controlling of me and didn't like it if I was out of his sight for long. I wanted to play out in the street with Emma but Charlie would never let me. I was allowed to play in the garden, as long as I was with my brother and sister, but he wouldn't let me out to play at Emma's house.

Still, Brownies was nice – they held it in the church hall at the bottom of our road and we'd play games, learn songs and once we even put on a play. It was Sleeping Beauty and I was the Queen, except I forgot my lines on the day! I was amazed – I had made a mistake and yet there weren't any consequences. I had forgotten my lines and nobody told me off or hit me.

I could laugh when I was at Brownies. I was free and happy there. But as the time approached for us to go home, I'd shrink back into myself. I knew what I had to go home to and I didn't like it.

Back home, Mum was still recovering from her treatment for cancer. When she wasn't drugged up on strong painkillers, she'd be shouting at me or having a go at Charlie.

Mum wasn't well enough to do anything round the house so I was still working hard to make sure everything was okay. I'd help get the kids out of bed and ready for school, help Charlie clean up the house, wash the pots, clean the kitchen, tidy the bedrooms, vacuum the floors, put the rubbish out. And all before school.

It meant I was always late – usually about an hour after the bell had rung. This didn't matter to Charlie, though, in fact he preferred it when I was in the house where he could keep an eye on me.

He also took me out of school a lot, making up fake doctor's appointments as an excuse to pick me up early. Then he'd take me to the pub with him where I played in the kids' area outside while he drank. He made sure I was always with him – maybe he worried that I would tell somebody or perhaps he just wanted complete control over me, I don't know. It was probably a little of both.

My new school knew that my mum was ill and that I was helping out at home, so they understood…at first. But then they started to notice that I'd changed – I had stopped speaking to people and was no longer the chatty, lively girl they had known.

They raised their concerns with Charlie but of course he just told them I was upset because of my mum! He had a way with people – he could tell them the sky was green and they'd believe him. At parents' evenings, they would sometimes invite the children to go along, but it was only Charlie who went with me, and whenever I was asked a question, he'd answer for me.

The teachers did try but by now I'd learned that whenever I stepped out of line, I would be made to pay for it at home. So I kept quiet.

'So what do you like to do in your spare time, Tina?' they'd ask gently.

'Oh, she likes lots of things,' Charlie would jump in. 'Reading, swimming, going out with her mates.'

Mates? What mates? It was a joke! My only friend was Emma, and I could only play with her at Brownies. Aside from her, I didn't have any friends and I never went out, not even on the street. And everybody knew this. Even the school knew because I didn't ever sit with a group of people or walk around with anyone. I was always on my own. But I wouldn't contradict Charlie in front of my teachers. He had total power over my life.

One time, Charlie got caught. He had cornered me in the living room when he thought everyone was out and he started having sex with me on the settee. I desperately tried to empty my mind, but then I heard a huge crash and I looked up to see that a cup of tea had been smashed against the wall.

Then I heard footsteps leaving the house and a door slamming. Someone had seen! Who was it? Maybe now it would all be over!

Charlie quickly got up and told me to get dressed, then I was sent up to my room. I honestly thought on that day it would all be over. Now somebody knew! It wasn't a secret any more and it wasn't my fault they'd found out.

Day after day I sat on the armchair by the window, scanning up and down the road, waiting for someone to come and take me away from that house, waiting for someone to rescue me. But no one ever came and the abuse just went on. When I finally accepted that no one was coming, all hope faded from me – I didn't think my life was ever going to change.

Later that year Charlie announced to us kids that we were all going on holiday to Blackpool.

'It's going to be fun,' he beamed. 'We're going to stay in a caravan and visit the arcades on the pier and enjoy ourselves. Your mum deserves a holiday after all she's been through.'

But I just couldn't get excited – even though I'd never been on holiday before, and Blackpool would have been the furthest I'd ever ventured from home. The problem was that Charlie would be there and being anywhere with Charlie was a nightmare.

The next day we sped down the motorway in Charlie's black Ford. Charlie drove, Mum was in the passenger seat holding Daniel while me, Lisa and Paul were crammed in the back – the other two were messing about but I just stared blankly out of the window.

At the campsite, the manager led us to an old, long caravan carpeted with an old, seventies style brown flowery design.

There were two bedrooms at one end with bunk beds and in the middle of the living room there was a dining table that converted into a bed. Against the wall in the living room was a large red settee covered by orange cushions.

Charlie organised the sleeping arrangements. 'Lisa and Paul can have the bedrooms,' he told my mum. 'Tina can sleep on the couch and we'll have the dining table bed.'

While Mum and Charlie unloaded the car, Lisa and I went off exploring – we found loads of hay bales covered in black bin liners and we clambered up and down on them until Mum called us in for tea.

She'd made fish fingers and chips and we wolfed them down as Lisa babbled excitedly about the hay bales.

*

Later that night, Charlie woke me up by getting into my bed. Mum was fast asleep, not two feet away in the bed next to us. He got on top of me, put his hand over my mouth then started having sex with me. You could feel the caravan moving while he was doing it but nobody woke up. I had tears coming down the side of my face but Charlie's hand stopped me making a sound while he held himself up with his other arm.

After about half an hour he took his hand away from my mouth, threw the cover back over me and sat on the edge of the bed that he shared with my mum. The crying now broke out of me in big gasping sobs and it woke Mum up. She opened her eyes and looked me over coldly.

'Why are you crying?' she said.

And before I could reply Charlie said, 'Oh, she's had a bad dream.'

Mum sighed, turned over and went back to sleep.

Charlie climbed back into bed next to my mum, looked at me sternly then went to sleep. I lay there all night crying.

The next night the same thing happened and on day three, Charlie took me out. He left Mum in the caravan with the other kids and he took me onto the front in Blackpool where he bought me clothes, shoes and toffees.

It was his way of buying my silence. But he didn't have to. The threats were enough to stop me from spilling the beans. By now I was terrified of him. I'd heard it often enough and I believed every word. *If I told anyone, he'd kill me. If I told anyone, he'd kill me.*

Besides, I no longer wanted anything from him. Before the abuse started, I loved the fact that Charlie treated me to clothes and sweets – I thought it showed he loved me as a father loves a daughter. But now it just made me feel sick.

When we first went to live with Charlie, I became a happy little girl, but now I was in a worse state than I ever had been; I was an introverted creature, full of fear. Sleep became a blessing: I could close my eyes and dream and forget everything. For that short amount of time I was in my own little world. Then I'd wake up and for a tiny second it felt like everything was great. But then I'd realise that I was back in my own bed, back in hell, and I knew I had to get through the whole day just to be able to get to bed at night and go to sleep and forget about it all again.

One day I asked Lisa if she wanted to run away with me.

'All right,' she said, thinking it would be a great adventure.

So we packed a bag with some clothes, her favourite teddy, and a pack of muffins from the kitchen cupboard and crept out of the house. We got as far as the end of the street before I realised we had nowhere to go.

Where could we run to? We didn't even have any money to get on a bus. I nearly cried with frustration. But I didn't want to upset Lisa so I opened our case and we ate a muffin each before walking back home. No one even noticed we'd been gone.

At times, I even looked forward to going to school, just to be out of the house and away from Charlie and my mum. Even so, I hated it when I was there. I'd creep along the corridors during break times, hoping nobody would see me to shout abuse at me. By now I'd taken to comfort eating as a way of filling the void of loneliness and misery inside. I loved biscuits and chocolates and sweets and, inevitably, I put on weight. The other kids called me 'fatty' and constantly teased me for being big. But I found a way to make friends, if only for a short while. I started stealing.

At first it was only one or two pounds here and there – I'd take the money out of Charlie's trousers when they were on the floor and go to the shops where I'd buy chocolates and sweets. Then I'd give them away to other kids at break times. It's sad but for those few minutes I felt popular and happy. I wasn't the miserable, fat girl who sat on her own any more – I was the kid with the free sweets. They were using me, it's true, but I was using them too. And besides, it wasn't my money so I didn't care.

Quickly, I realised the more sweets I could give away, the more other children would like me. So I started taking more and more money from the house – a fiver here, a tenner there. On the way to school I'd stop off at the sweetshop and load up on boxes of liquorice, strawberry bonbons, Kit Kats, penny toffees and white chewing gum balls.

One Sunday morning, while the whole family was still asleep, I climbed onto a chair in the living room so that I could reach the top cupboard where Mum and Charlie hid the money jar. I carefully removed a ten-pound note, then I put it in my bag and quietly, so as not to wake anyone, left the house. My plan was to buy a load of sweets from the shop so I could take them into school the next day.

At the shop, I saw a girl from school. Nia was also an outcast like me – she was bullied because she wore glasses – so we had a fun morning that day walking round the shop, choosing how to spend my parents' ten pounds. I picked out two big bars of Dairy Milk and a few other sweets, then I went home, eager to hide my loot in my bedroom cupboard where no one would find them. But when I got in, Charlie was already in the living room.

'Where have you been?' he snarled.

'I just went to the shop.'

'Well, where did you get the money from?

'I had some left over from the week – you gave it me for school.'

'You're lying!' he yelled. 'I know the money's gone cos it's not in the pot.'

That was it – my heart dropped into my stomach and I bolted out of the room. He'd caught me out in a lie and I was scared to death. I ran up the stairs and threw myself down on the bed. Charlie had leapt off the settee and was quick on my heels. The door flew open and I shook with fear.

'I'm sorry, I'm sorry,' I cried, the tears pouring down my cheeks. 'I won't do it again.'

'Too bloody right you won't!' he roared then he got hold of me, wheeled me round and whacked me on the back. Hard. It was a real punch and it knocked the breath out of me.

Then he bent me over his knee and started smacking my bum over and over again – I thought it was never going to stop. Finally, when he'd had enough, he threw me back down on the bed. I was so sore I could barely move.

'You do that again and I'll kill you.'

It stopped me – for about three weeks. And then I did it again, but this time I took twenty pounds. I was rebelling. I'd got to the point where I didn't care what happened to me. As far as I was concerned, life couldn't get any worse. Charlie was abusing me, my mum hated me – what more could they do to make my life miserable?

So I took a twenty-pound note – the only problem was I didn't get a chance to go the shop and spend it because Charlie found it underneath my pillow in my bedroom.

I nabbed the cash at about 6 p.m. on Thursday as I planned to take it into school the next day and spend it on sweets but I didn't have time. I went to bed about nine and put it under my pillow. I thought nobody would notice it there. But then Charlie came into the bedroom.

'Turn off the TV,' he said. 'It's your bedtime and you have to go to sleep. Your mum's in bed asleep.'

And the moment he said that, I knew what he was there for.

'Take off your pyjama bottoms,' he ordered, quietly but menacingly. 'And pull up your top.'

Charlie wanted to touch me and make me feel him too so he fumbled around with my chest before putting himself inside me.

But as I turned my head to the side so I wouldn't have to look at him, the pillow slipped and there it was, staring at him – the twenty-pound note.

He didn't say anything – he just carried on.

Afterwards, he got up, took the money and said, 'Get up. Now.'

I went to stand and as I did so I felt an almighty thwack across the face.

'You're going to regret that,' he said, as I held my burning cheek.

The next morning Charlie didn't speak to me – he didn't say one word. Just gave me this horrible, nasty look. I went to school as usual, but couldn't concentrate on my lessons – I spent the whole day in a state of fear and terror. What was he going to do now?

When I came home from school Charlie put me in the car and we drove to the police station. A police officer took me and Charlie into a room and sat me at a chair and table. Then the officer towered over me, not speaking for a bit. Just looking at me.

Finally he spoke. 'It's a crime to steal, did you know that, Tina?'

I nodded my head, terrified.

'It's a crime,' he continued, 'whether it's a little bit of money or something from a shop, it's still a crime. People get put away in prison for taking things that don't belong to them. You're not too young to go to prison for stealing.'

I was scared to death – I thought he was going to lock me up in the cells. And yes, it did stop me taking money from Charlie and my mum from that point.

Of course, nobody told me that it was a crime to rape your stepdaughter. Nobody took Charlie down to a police station to threaten him with being locked up in a cell.

I knew stealing was wrong. But in my heart I also knew that what Charlie was doing was wrong. Where was my police officer? Why couldn't they stop him?

Chapter 4
Alone

When I was eleven, I started at a mixed high school where there were girls and boys together – it felt strange mingling with boys, especially older ones. Sometimes I'd eavesdrop on the big girls talking to each other about 'going with' a boy and I started to realise that what Charlie was doing to me was what other girls and boys did together. But not with their dads.

Of course, Charlie didn't like me talking to boys so he took me out of that school and put me into an all-girls school. There, they gave us sex education classes – they talked to us about sex, condoms, and penises. All the other girls thought it was a big joke and spent most of the class in fits of giggles. But I had nothing to laugh about. *That's happening to me!* I wanted to scream. But I couldn't say anything.

I walked around in a cloud of shame. I was ashamed of myself, of my mum and Charlie, and especially of my body. I felt it was dirty because of what Charlie was doing to me so getting undressed for PE was horrible. Even in the girls school I found PE really difficult. I was terrified of taking off my clothes. The thought of getting undressed just made me feel sick and disgusted with myself. I couldn't bear taking a shower in front of thirty other people. I thought that if they saw my body that somehow they'd know. They'd see where he had been and they'd think I was disgusting too. So I made up excuses not to do it. At first, it was easy. I used to pretend I was ill or I'd say I had a really bad stomach ache. I could make myself cry so it wasn't hard to convince the teachers that I was in pain. All I had to do was think of something Charlie had done and then I'd just burst into tears. Crying was my habit because I was actually upset most of the time.

When Charlie realised I had a weakness with PE, that's when the bribery started.

In the morning, he'd say: 'Come on, get on top of me, and you can stay off school for the day.' So I did. It was a desperate situation. I detested school so much for its routine humiliation, and in many ways what Charlie was doing to me had become normality, so giving him what he wanted seemed the easier option. I was so numb to his actions by now, but not to those of the school bullies. Then, one day after one of my rare appearances at a PE lesson, I started my period. I had just turned twelve and as usual was the last person to leave the changing room when I felt my knickers getting damp. I went to the toilet and saw the blood there so I stuffed some tissue in my pants and went to the Head of Year, who was a really nice lady. I didn't know how to tell her but she took one look at my face and guessed,

'Come on,' she said kindly. 'Let's take you to the nurse to get some sanitary towels. Don't worry – it's perfectly normal.'

Later that day, I told Charlie and he didn't come into my room that night. In fact he avoided me for the next seven days.

'*Brilliant*,' I thought to myself. '*I wish I had my period every day!*'

Plus, it gave me another excuse to get out of PE. Unfortunately, I had to do PE twice a week and the teachers started to pick up that something wasn't right. How many times could I say I was having a bad period before they started to get suspicious? So Charlie started writing sick notes for me – he said I couldn't do PE because I had a hospital appointment, or I had a bad leg or I'd hurt my shoulder.

They always believed him for some reason – he had this way. And he could convince almost anybody. Once he turned up to my school completely drunk, demanding I be taken out of lessons immediately. And they let him! He said I had a doctor's appointment but that was a lie. He just took me to the pub again.

I find it remarkable now that no one ever got to the bottom of my problem. I was overweight, lonely, bullied and when I wasn't skipping classes, my dad was taking me out of school. The teachers must have suspected there was something going wrong in my life. But they never asked me outright whether there was a problem, and if a teacher ever asked me about stuff at home, I would always lie. I'd tell them how good things were and how happy I was. I told people I got on well with my mum and I loved her to bits, even though I absolutely hated her guts. And when they asked if I liked having Charlie for a stepdad, I always said, 'Yeah, it's really nice.'

But while I was saying all this, I felt like throwing up. I was too ashamed to tell the truth. I didn't want anybody to know my secrets. What would people think of me if they knew?

A day came when we moved to yet another new place not far from a big park. That was a nice four-bedroom house with a huge garden and of course I had my own room. Charlie always made sure I had my own room – that way he could do what he wanted and there'd never be any witnesses.

By now, Mum had started to get a little better – still, she wasn't any easier to live with. She was always cross and it was usually about the same thing.

Charlie had been sleeping downstairs all this time and was too busy with me to pay her much attention.

'Why won't you touch me?' she'd shriek at him. 'Don't you love me no more?'

The arguments would start up and then at some point she'd walk out, just like she did in the old days.

She'd take me and my brothers and sister with her and I'd enjoy a few, blissful, Charlie-free days.

Life was back to how it had once been and in those periods without Charlie, I could relax for a few days at my auntie Tanya's house or with Mum's friends. I felt sure she would leave him for real eventually and every time she packed our bags and announced 'Come on, we're going' I hoped it would be for good this time.

But for some reason she always went back to him. Maybe he apologised or begged her to come home – he was probably terrified that he couldn't control me when I was out of his clutches.

Every time she left it was for the same reason.

'He doesn't see me in the same way,' she'd cry to my auntie Tanya. 'He doesn't fancy me like he did when we first met. It's cos I've been ill.'

But Charlie was crafty – he found a way to get my mum back. He moved his bed back upstairs and obviously showed her some attention again. So we ended up back at Charlie's.

I thought I was never going to escape.

One day I was doing my homework on the living room floor while Charlie lounged on the settee, flicking through the TV channels when we heard a knock at the door.

I went to open it and saw three people standing there – a policeman and two women.

'We'd like to speak to your mum and dad,' said the policeman.

'Had they done something wrong? Maybe they've been stealing,' I thought, recalling my last encounter with the police.

I went and got Mum, who was in the kitchen making tea, and she showed them into the living room.

'Do you mind sending Tina out for this?' one of the ladies turned to my mum. 'We need to talk in private.'

'Oh god, it's me!' I panicked. *'I've done something wrong and now I'm in trouble.'*

I felt sick with fear but Mum ordered me upstairs then shut the door behind her. But instead I sat on the bottom step and listened to what they said.

'Mr and Mrs Jenkins, I'm from social services and my colleague here is from the NSPCC. We're here because we've had an anonymous call. The caller said they had concerns that Tina, your eldest daughter, is being abused.'

My stomach lurched and I could feel my heart beating so fast I wondered if they could hear it in the living room. *'Here we go,'* I thought. *'Someone's seen it; it's going to come out. It's all going to be over!'*

The next voice I heard was my mum's.

She sounded shocked. 'What are you talking about? That sort of thing wouldn't happen here! Charlie wouldn't do anything like that.'

She was so convincing I half believed her myself!

'That might well be the case,' said one of the women. 'But we do have to investigate this phone call we've had.'

At that point Charlie chipped in. 'It's not true. I wouldn't touch Tina. It's a load of lies. I'd never do anything like that. I love her to bits and I'd never hurt her or do anything like that to her.'

He sounded genuinely distressed and angry – I just wanted to cry. I knew at that point they would believe him.

My mum meanwhile continued to scoff at the suggestion. 'What a load of nonsense!' she exclaimed. 'I don't know where you got that idea from!'

Between Charlie and mum, they must have been quite convincing because after a while, the policeman and the two women just upped and left. I heard them getting ready to go so I climbed the stairs and hid round the corner on the landing. I watched them disappear down the front path, and that was it. We never heard from them again.

Nobody talked to me, nobody asked me anything. The thing is, looking back now, I don't think I'd have told them what was happening even if they *had* asked me. I was just too scared. It had been going on now for so long and Charlie had told me so many times that he'd kill me if I told anyone, I was in a state of constant fear.

I believed everything Charlie said and was convinced if I ever told anybody they would hate me and think I was disgusting. They'd blame me. Even now I have to fight the belief that everything that happened to me as a child was my own fault. I know I was innocent and that Charlie was the criminal, but it's hard to believe that in your heart when you're told you are to blame so many times.

After the police and the lady left, Mum slammed the door and went back to making tea – she didn't come to see me and I didn't talk to her either but she was different with Charlie that night. Whenever he asked her something she refused to answer him back – it was like she was in a mood with him.

I don't know why, but we didn't hear any more about the visit from the police. Maybe they believed Mum and Charlie. One thing I do know is that it didn't take long for Charlie to abuse me again. In fact the abuse became even worse. He started taking more and more risks.

Like always, if I wanted a note to get out of PE in the morning, he'd insist I give him sex first. But there were many occasions, in the morning, when he'd have sex with me in the living room. He'd just put a chair in front of the door to stop anyone coming in.

One morning Charlie said, 'Right, do you want to stay off school today?'

I knew what he wanted. He told me to get undressed and get on top of him. Then he sat on the chair but we got interrupted by the sound of someone trying to get into the living room. Mum.

He jumped up, told me to hurry up and get dressed and pulled on his pants and trousers. Then, calm as you like, he moved the chair away from the door while I sat on the settee.

Mum came in. 'What's this chair doing in front of the door?' she snapped.

'I was cleaning behind the chair so I had to move it,' said Charlie quickly.

And that was that – she believed him. She didn't say anything else, just went into the kitchen to make herself a drink and went back upstairs to bed. I couldn't believe it – there wasn't so much as a duster in that living room but she didn't look twice!

But then I suppose Mum wasn't really herself at the time. Although she'd beaten the cancer she'd developed epilepsy and had been put on strong drugs that made her sleepy much of the time. When she wasn't arguing with Charlie, or leaving him, she spent her days asleep. If she noticed anything or had her suspicions, she never asked me. I assumed she just didn't know.

The only time I heard much from her was when I had to listen to her moan that Charlie wasn't sleeping with her, while I was being forced to sleep with him to get anything that I wanted.

If I wanted money to go to the shop, I had to give him sex, if I wanted to get off school, I had to give him sex. It was a constant thing. It came to the point where I just did it because that was all I'd ever known. In my mind I just had to get it over and done with and then I could go out or get some money. I felt more like a prostitute than a daughter.

That went on until I was thirteen when Mum walked out for real. Charlie and Mum had had a really big argument while I was in school and I came home to find she'd packed her bags. Paul and Lisa were standing next to her, each holding a bag of their own.

'I'm going,' she said to me. 'But I'm not taking you.'

She left Daniel too, who was three by now, but I didn't think much of it at the time. I'm not sure why she didn't take Daniel with her though – perhaps a small child was too much trouble for her, or Charlie wouldn't let her. Mum had left me before, so that wasn't anything new. She'd walked out on so many occasions that I just assumed she'd come back. I didn't even want to go with her and I didn't feel particularly hurt that she didn't want me. I hated my mum for the way she'd been with me all my life.

But Mum never came back and I was stuck in the house with Charlie and Daniel. Now I became like a real mum to my little brother – I fed him, changed him, dressed him, took him to nursery before I went to school and picked him up again on my way back. His nursery school actually started thinking I was his mother because even though I was now thirteen, I looked a lot older.

After Mum left things started to get a lot worse with Charlie – he was angry a lot of the time and he'd shout at me a lot or smack me. And it was never the kind of smack that you'd give a kid – it was a real punch. He'd hit me for anything – for answering back, for not cleaning the house properly or, god forbid, if I said no to him. When he wanted to have sex and I said no then he'd hit me and I was forced to do it anyway.

Meanwhile Mum and my brother and sister moved from one place to another and eventually she got a council flat of her own in a large hostel. I'd often go to visit them at weekends but there was never any question of me moving in there – in her own way Mum abused me just as much as Charlie. It was mental torture. While I was at Mum's I met a girl who lived across the road. At twenty, Jayne was much older than me but we got on well and one Saturday night we got all dressed up and she took me to a nightclub in town. I was so scared we were going to get caught but we walked in and nobody questioned me about my age. It was brilliant. I danced all night and I loved it.

Of course I couldn't tell Charlie where I'd been. He was always very suspicious after I came back from Mum's and he'd question me about what I was up to and who I'd spoken to. I had to lie all the time so that I didn't upset him. He didn't want me talking to boys – that's why he'd taken me out of the mixed secondary school.

At the club, it had been strange seeing all these older boys and girls going around together, holding hands and kissing. But then I realised that that was how it was supposed to be – I even started wondering if I would ever have a boyfriend myself. *'Don't be silly,'* I'd tell myself. *'You'll never have a boyfriend. Charlie won't let you.'*

It was true – Charlie was horribly jealous. Even if we were walking down the road and I looked at a boy, Charlie would give me a telling off. So, mostly I lied. If I lied to Charlie I didn't get into trouble. Everything about my life became a lie. It was my survival mechanism. I lied to the teachers at school about my life and I lied to Charlie about everything else. And I was better at it than Mum – I'd learned from her mistakes that you had to remember what you'd said so you didn't get caught out.

There were times I'd pretend to Charlie that I was going to school but instead I'd get on the bus to go and see Mum. It's not that I wanted to be with her particularly – she was still the same with me, bullying, mean and nasty. But I liked to see Lisa and Paul.

As bad as my life was with Charlie, I felt sorry for my brother and sister. Mum just couldn't look after them properly because she was drugged up on medication so much of the time. So they were basically left to fend for themselves and the house was a filthy mess. Looking back now, perhaps I could have tried to help them, but realistically, what could I do? I was only thirteen and in a terrible situation myself. And any contact I had had with the authorities showed me that I was unlikely to be believed. I had been told so many times I was worthless, so who on earth would feel it was worth their time to help me?

Strangely, even though Mum hated animals, she let Lisa and Paul have a dog. It wasn't housetrained and they let it poo on the kitchen floor and wee all over the carpets – it was revolting. I couldn't eat anything when I went to Mum's house because the thought of what the food might have touched made me feel sick.

Mum never did any laundry so my brother and sister went to school in the same clothes they'd had on for days. The schools began to notice they were being neglected and it wasn't long before social services become involved.

One time Charlie and I drove over to Mum's place to pick up Lisa and Paul who were due to be staying with us for the weekend. But when we got there the front door was wide open. We went inside to see Mum sparked out on the couch with the TV on but no sign of my brother and sister.

I tried everything to wake Mum up but she was out of it – I shouted at her, shook her and even threw water over her but she was on so much medication she wouldn't wake up so we had to go and find the kids.

Paul was just six at the time and one of Mum's neighbours told us they'd seen him at the golf course round the corner. My sister, who was eight, was three miles away at the park with her mates. We found her pretty quickly but spent the whole day driving around looking for my brother. We went down to the golf course but couldn't find Paul there – one of the golfers said they'd seen him riding off on his bike. So we hunted round the estate near where my mum lived, walking down the alleyways you couldn't drive down.

Finally we caught sight of him in the car park on his bike.

'Paul!' Charlie shouted. 'Get here, *now*!'

Paul took one look at us, and sprinted away on his bike.

'You go down there,' Charlie pointed at an alley-way, 'and I'll go down here and we can grab the little bastard.'

As ever, I was too scared of Charlie not to obey him. I ran down the alleyway, and almost came face to face with Paul, who turned and pedalled away from me as fast as he could.

I lost Paul but Charlie managed to find him and forced him into a corner where there was no escape. 'You little toe rag,' I heard him shout, 'think you can get away from me, do you?'

As I came running up behind them I saw Paul throw down his bike and try to climb the fence to get away from Charlie. But he wasn't fast enough.

Charlie grabbed him by the scruff of his neck, dragged him to the ground and started hitting Paul on his back. 'Think you can get away from me?' he repeated, between great, whacking hits that seemed to lift my poor little brother's body off the ground. 'Think again, you little shit.'

That night I heard Paul sobbing in the bath and my heart went out to him. But seeing what Charlie had done also made me more fearful. I knew that's what would happen to me if I ever tried to escape, only worse. Much worse.

The next day Paul had handprints on his back and when he went home to Mum, she took him to the hospital and reported Charlie to social services. Charlie was interviewed about the marks on Paul's back – he told them all he'd done was slap him a couple of times, and, as usual, they believed him.

By then Mum had been deemed unfit to look after Lisa and Paul so they were put on care orders and a few months later they were taken away from her.

I'll never forget that day – I was there when the social workers came to take them.

Mum was at the door, crying her eyes out, being held back by a social worker while the kids were bundled into the back of a car and driven away. Mum just collapsed on the doorstep in tears – and they left her like that.

After Lisa and Paul were taken away I still went to Mum's place occasionally. She had a neighbour whose son Kieron was about my age, so without my brother and sister there I ended up chatting to him a lot.

'Do you like school?' he asked, as we sat on the wall, sharing a Toffee Crisp.

'Yeah, it's great,' I lied. What was I going to tell him? That everybody hated me and I was bullied? 'I love it – I've got tonnes of friends and the teachers really like me.'

He nodded. 'You know, my mum and dad have split up,' he said. 'I think my dad likes your mum.'

I giggled – Kieron was really nice. We spent ages just chatting about the TV programmes we liked and daring each other to spy on our parents. I wanted to be truthful with him but I couldn't. I wanted him to like me, and to think I was normal like him. Outside of my family, Kieron was the first lad I'd talked to in my entire life! There was nothing sexual in it, nothing bad. We just used to sit up all night chatting about different things.

One night, he was telling me all about how his mum and dad used to argue a lot and how much he hated it and at that moment, I felt like telling him everything. But over the years I'd learned to think before I spoke – what would happen? What would the consequences be? I played it over in my mind and kept coming back to the same conclusion.

Charlie would find out and then he'd kill me, that's what would happen.

So I kept quiet – but talking to Kieron that night made me feel different. Something clicked into place and I realised that what Charlie was doing was wrong. And I didn't want it any more.

I went home one night after spending the weekend talking to Kieron and when Charlie wanted sex I found I was different with him.

'No,' I said defiantly. 'I don't want to do this.'

He could sense something had changed. I'd never spoken to him like this before.

'What's wrong with you?' he asked. 'What's happened? Why are you being funny with me?'

'I don't want this no more,' I said again, this time more firmly. 'I've had enough. I want you to leave me alone.'

That was it. He grabbed hold of me, pushed me onto the settee, slapped me so hard that my head spun round and then he came up to me, holding up a threatening finger to my face and growled: 'You'll never get away. You'll never leave. The only way you'll get away from me is in a body bag.'

The look on his face put the fear of God into me. Even now I can close my eyes and see that anger on his face. I knew that he meant what he said; I knew that he would kill me rather than let me go.

Then he got up and walked out. I sat there shaking and crying. I was so upset. I just wanted to end things. I'd had enough. But I had nowhere to go and no one I could tell. I really didn't want to live any more. From that point on, I knew the only way I would get away from him was if I was dead.

Chapter 5

Pregnant

There was a woman called Ruth who lived in the same hostel as my mum and she had ten kids, the youngest of which was six months old. So whenever I used to visit Mum on the weekends, I'd always go down to see Ruth and take the little boy out to the park in the pram. It was lovely – I'd rearrange his blankets, play Peek-a-Boo with him and generally coo and fuss over him as he smiled and giggled in the sunlight. If I picked him up he'd clutch my chest and I loved feeling the tiny nails on his little fingers and toes.

'*I'd love to have a baby,*' I thought to myself then. A sweet little baby with chubby fingers who'd claw at my chest, who I could love and who would love me back.

Just pure love, without hate, bitterness or pain. Little did I know that my wish was about to be granted.

It was during a week I was off school when I started to feel unwell. I'd gone to Mum's for the weekend but on the Saturday morning I woke up with a sick feeling in the pit of my stomach. As I swung my legs out of bed, I was suddenly hit by a wave of nausea and ran to the bathroom to throw up.

I dragged myself back to bed then lay there feeling rotten before my mum came in. She'd heard me puking in the bathroom and she stood looking at me from the doorway, her head to one side, brows furrowed.

'What's up with you?' she demanded.

'I don't know,' I replied. 'I just feel really sick and I'm dead tired.'

'Well, you could be pregnant,' she said matter-of-factly. 'Let's find out, shall we?'

Mum went off to the chemist's right away and when she came back she told me how to use the kit – I had to pee onto a little stick and show her the results.

I was terrified of what the test might show – what if I was pregnant? What was I going to say? I couldn't tell anyone who the father was! And of course, there had been no one else other than Charlie – I had never come close to being intimate with a boy.

'Well, it's positive!' Mum announced a few minutes later and with that, I burst into tears. For the first time in my life, Mum showed me some compassion.

'Oh, come here,' she soothed as she put her arms around me. 'It'll be okay. Don't worry about it. Just tell me – who's the father?'

'I...uh...I...I don't know,' I managed to gasp between sobs. 'Please don't tell Charlie!'

Mum agreed to keep the pregnancy a secret from Charlie and for the next couple of days my emotions swung wildly between elation and depression. It might have been the hormones kicking in but one minute, I'd be delighted. A little baby! My own baby! I fantasised about our lives together – taking my baby to the park, walking it through the town in its stroller, cuddling it at night and all the lovely times we would share together. But within minutes that fantasy world would be replaced by a nightmare as I remembered who the father was and I was filled with shame and disgust. I couldn't have Charlie's baby! The very idea was sickening. I hated the thought of his child growing inside me…but then at least I'd soon have somebody to love and, finally, somebody to love me back. I couldn't settle on one feeling.

Of course it didn't take Charlie long to notice that something was different about me. The morning sickness carried on when I got home from mum's and I was more tired than usual. I'd lie on the settee, staring blankly at the telly and had barely enough energy to get through all my cooking and cleaning duties.

A few days later Charlie took me to his local pub, and I told him I wasn't feeling well.

'Right, well why don't you go to the chemist and ask them to do a pregnancy test?'

My heart started pounding – he was going to find out!

Still, I couldn't argue about it. I went to the chemist's along the road and as I was walking, I tried to figure out what I was going to tell them. I knew I couldn't give them my real name and age so I made up a fake name, address and date of birth.

They did the test right there and when the result came back positive, as I knew it would, the chemist took down all my fake details. Then he handed me the pregnancy stick and a piece of paper to take to my GP.

My hands were shaking as I walked back into the pub – but with a pretence of calm, I just handed Charlie the piece of paper without a word, walked back to my usual seat in the corner and started flicking through my *Smash Hits* magazine, drinking my Coke like nothing had happened.

Charlie just sat there drinking, apparently deep in thought. Then he came over to me and started talking in a low voice.

'Right, you're not getting rid of it so you can forget about that,' he started. 'Now, I want you to think of a boy's name. It doesn't matter what name. You have to tell everybody that you went out to a party with a friend, you got drunk and you slept with some boy. You don't know where he lives and you don't know his last name, just his first. That's what you have to say.'

I sat there nodding in silence, but all the while my head was spinning.

Out with a friend? To a party? I had only ever gone out once, with Jayne, and had danced the night away with her. I'd never even touched a drink. Who would believe me?

But that night I played over the story in my mind – yes, I'd gone to a party. It was a late-night party in a friend's house. I let my imagination go and the scene just started to play out like a film in my head. The music was on loud, the room filled with smoke and there were boys who gave me vodka and Coke.

I got chatting to a nice guy called Alex. He was tall with dark brown hair and green eyes. I started to picture him – the baggy jeans he wore, the gold chain around his neck. After a while he put his hand around my waist and pulled me to him, telling me I was beautiful and he wanted to kiss me...

The fantasy took off from there and from that night I started to really believe the story Charlie had made up for me. Why? Because I so wanted it to be true; I really wanted to be a normal girl and to be with a good-looking boy who loved me and thought I was special. I didn't want to be pregnant with Charlie's baby so I imagined that the real father was a handsome dark-haired boy called Alex.

The following weekend I was back at my mum's house, armed with the fantasy that was now as real to me as the actual pregnancy.

'So who's the father?' Mum demanded as soon as I walked in the door.

I didn't hesitate. 'It's a boy called Alex. I went to a party with Jayne from round the corner, and he was there. We were all drinking, vodka and Coke, and I got drunk. He took me upstairs and we slept together.'

She looked at me hard then, but I didn't blink. I'm not sure if she believed me but Charlie had already dreamt up a plan to make the whole lie appear real.

'He's picking me up tonight,' I went on blithely. 'Yeah, he's got a car and he says he's going to take me out.'

'Well, how nice for you,' Mum sneered.

So later that evening, just as Charlie directed, I made a big show of ironing my favourite white shirt, blow-drying my hair and painting my nails.

Mum eyed me suspiciously from the settee as I sat on the living-room floor, make-up mirror in hand, carefully drawing an outline of black round my eyes.

'So where does he live then, this Alex?'

'I don't know, Mum!'

'How old is he?'

'He's eighteen. He says he's going to pick me up round the corner.'

'Right, well just be back before twelve.'

It was typical. It was one of the few times my mum had shown any interest in me, now, when her quizzing me was the last thing I needed. So I sat watching *Blind Date* with Mum until the clock hit nine, then I dutifully left the house and walked to the end of the road where Charlie was waiting round the corner in his black car.

My heart fell as he drove us to the deserted, unlit car park in the local park. I could guess what was coming next – this wasn't going to be an easy couple of hours driving round the block. As soon as he'd parked up and switched the engine off, he undid his seatbelt and turned to me, his hand fumbling urgently with his trouser buttons.

'Come on,' he said. 'You're here now – play with me!'

I felt sick as a dog but I had no choice – if I refused I'd only get a beating. I had hoped that my pregnancy would mean that he left me alone, but it never did. So I played with his penis as he leaned back against the car window, eyes shut.

Next, he made me get into the backseat, straddle him and have sex with him. Twice. I felt disgusted.

Later on, he drove me back to Mum's.

'Right, tell her you went with Alex to the pub where you met some friends and had a few drinks. Think you can manage that?'

I nodded dumbly.

Back at Mum's I repeated Charlie's story word for word. Mum didn't care that I was telling her I'd been to a pub underage, and she just shrugged when I told her the story Charlie had concocted for me. I don't know how she could have bought that rubbish – I didn't have a drop of alcohol on my breath. She was back to her usual self.

*

For eight weeks Charlie kept up the fantasy of my dates with the imaginary Alex – and every Friday and Saturday night I had to go through the pantomime of getting all dolled up for meeting my boyfriend when actually my stepdad was forcing me to have sex with him in his car.

Then Charlie turned round one morning before I left for Mum's and gave me a new story. 'Right, he's split up with you. Alex dumped you and he doesn't want anything to do with you or the baby. Got it?'

Some part of me was relieved – no more sordid sex sessions with Charlie in his car, and no more lying to Mum about the imaginary places I'd been to with Alex. But at the same time, I was heartbroken. Alex had been my escape route, the way I could forget about my horrible situation.

I'd spent so many hours daydreaming about him and the time we'd spent together, it was hard to let him go. I'd imagined the long, romantic walks through the park, sitting watching the sunset in his car, holding hands in the rain and all the lovely things he said to me when we were alone.

I was constantly changing and improving him. Sometimes I'd imagine he was one of the boys from my old high school, other times he would be the boy I saw walking down the street. I gave him different faces, hairstyles and clothes, but the one constant factor in my fantasy was that he was kind to me, gentle and loving. Alex was my lifeline – and now Charlie was killing him off.

I wondered why – perhaps he realised that the fantasy could not be retained for ever, or perhaps, in some sick, twisted way he felt jealous. After all, everyone now assumed I had a boyfriend, a nice guy with a car. And that guy wasn't him.

Either way, without my imaginary Alex I felt bereft. I could not hide myself from the awful fact that I was carrying my stepdad's child and every day I woke up with a feeling of dread and horror. This tiny innocent life was growing inside me and though I wanted to love it, I was repulsed by the thought of who the father was.

I'd become even more isolated from the other girls at school. There was no one there who I could talk to. But things were about to change.

One lunchtime, I was walking up the hill to the canteen when Kate, one of the girls from my maths class, came up beside me. We weren't particularly friendly, but she wasn't one of the bullies, either. As we reached the dining hall, my appetite fled and I stopped short, just before the entrance.

'Aren't you coming in for dinner?' said Kate, questioningly.

'No,' I replied, my stomach now in knots. 'I'm not hungry.'

It was the first time I'd spoken all day and for some reason just hearing my own pathetic little voice made my eyes well up and I ran weeping from the canteen.

Kate came to find me as I sat in the back of a classroom next door.

'What's wrong?' she asked, concerned.

I couldn't keep it in any longer, I just blurted it out. 'I'm pregnant.'

'So, why are you crying?' she asked, gently. 'Don't you want to have the baby?'

I didn't know what to say. I couldn't tell her it was because I was pregnant with my stepdad's baby! So I just sat there, sobbing.

She sat down on the chair next to me and said, 'Don't worry – because I'm pregnant too.'

I was so shocked my head shot up from where it had been resting on my arms over the desk and I just stared at her.

'Yeah! Really!' she laughed. 'Come on. We'll go to the Head of Year and I'll be with you when you tell her.'

'I don't want to,' I wailed.

I was petrified of telling the school I was pregnant. I was scared of getting into trouble from them and scared of going home and getting into more trouble from Charlie. But Kate said that telling the teachers wasn't so bad and by now I was so confused I really didn't know what to do.

So we went to the Head of Year together and Kate announced, 'Tina's got something to say. She doesn't know what to do, she wants to talk.'

I sat down in a chair in the corner and again uttered those two small words that meant so much: 'I'm pregnant.'

The Head of Year was really nice about it. She didn't ask me who the father was, she just came and put her arms around me and said, 'Don't worry, things will be fine.'

She asked how far along I was and whether I'd told my parents.

When I told her I was four months gone and confirmed my parents knew, she went on, 'Well, look, you can't stay in school any more. It's not your fault but if you carried on in school and one of the other kids knocked you over in the corridor, there's a risk you could lose the baby. We're not insured against that kind of risk so we'll have to send you to a mother-and-baby unit.'

Kate nudged me. 'I'm going too. We'll be together.'

I managed a weak smile before fear engulfed me again. Now the school knew – how long before they told Charlie? Would I get into trouble for spilling the beans?

As it turned out, Charlie didn't seem to mind when school rang him up and said they were transferring me to the mother-and-baby unit.

They called him in the middle of the day and when I got home that night, he asked, 'Did you tell the school you're pregnant?'

I was shaking with fear. 'Yeah, I had to. One of the girls found out and she made me go to the Head of Year.'

'Okay,' he said.

And that was it. It was so confusing with Charlie – you never knew what to expect. He could be fine one minute and then blow up the next. I was constantly worried and sick with fear about how he was going to behave.

But Charlie thought everything would be fine. What he didn't know was that the school now had their suspicions about the identity of the father. After all, they saw me every day, they knew I didn't have friends and I didn't hang around with anybody. So they contacted social services with their concerns and once again, the wheels were in motion to try and get to the bottom of my situation.

Two weeks later I moved to the mother-and-baby unit with my new friend Kate. It was in a large building at the back of the local hospital and every morning and afternoon, the school sent taxis to collect us pregnant girls.

Our main classroom was a small room with a square table in the middle and chairs round the sides, and across the corridor, there was a tiny galley kitchen where we could make our own food and drinks. Further into the building, through a pair of big double doors, there was a larger room with a table where we had lessons like art and cookery.

Art lessons were great – I loved being creative and could draw quite well.

There were only three subjects we studied at the mother-and-baby unit – art, cookery and childcare. And once a week we were taken down the swimming baths where we splashed around in the water for an hour.

For once, I didn't feel self-conscious as I got ready for swimming. It wasn't like PE where there were thirty-odd girls running round in shorts. There were only four of us, all pregnant, and we were allowed to wear T-shirts over our costumes.

Then, at lunchtimes we'd all traipse down to the hospital canteen with our free lunch tickets and eat together.

Kate was only a month further along than me so we became quite good friends and after school we'd all be driven back home by car.

Perhaps I could have told Kate about my situation at home, but I had become so careful of what I could and couldn't say to people, that it just seemed impossible to me that I could trust her completely. The consequences of telling people would go round and round in my head. Would she tell someone else? Would she make fun of me? Would Charlie find out that I had told his secret, and what would happen then? I had seen what he had done to Paul when he had tried to run away, and that level of violence frightened me. I couldn't imagine any good would come out of telling people about Charlie and my horrific life at home – at best, I thought no one would believe me, or they would blame me, somehow, for the abuse I suffered. At worst I thought that Charlie would kill me. His threats and mind games had worked – I was under his thumb, even when he wasn't around. It was the same old, horrifying thoughts that plagued me every day.

However, at the mother-and-baby unit I could forget about Charlie and my cares for a while. I had friends, I had people who were in the same boat as me, and when I was there, I didn't feel alone. All in all, I loved it. It was probably the best school I ever went to and it never even occurred to me to bunk off.

One day Charlie took me and Daniel to the park – I was about five months gone by now and Daniel was three and a half. The park was just round the corner from where we lived, and Charlie and I sat on the grass by the car as Daniel peddled down the hill on his tricycle.

'I can't wait till this baby comes,' Charlie gushed, all excited.

'Uh, yeah,' I murmured, brushing my hand along the grass, trying not to look at him.

He seemed so happy since I got pregnant – but I hated hearing him talk about the little one growing inside me. It made me sick with disgust. By now we'd found out it was a boy and Charlie seemed so happy he couldn't stop going on about it. Still, it was a nice day and I was enjoying watching the leaves falling down from the trees.

Suddenly the quietness was pierced by an almighty shriek – Daniel!

Charlie sent me down to the gates where Daniel had been playing to find out what was wrong and the sight that met me when I got down there was so awful, I threw up on the spot. The thumb of his right hand had got caught in the bolt lock of the metal gate and the flesh of the whole tip had come away, revealing just the bone below. Daniel, terrified, started running back up the hill to Charlie while I lay on the grass, retching and crying.

Charlie remained calm – he even went down to the gates, picked up the tip of the thumb and put it in his pocket.

Then he took my jumper off me, wrapped it round Daniel's hand and bundled us both into the back of the car while he drove like a madman to the hospital.

Daniel was a gibbering wreck. 'Am I going to die?' he kept asking me over and over again.

I couldn't say a word. I was crying too much.

Afterwards, I wondered how I was ever going to be a mum. At the first sign of trouble, I'd panicked.

Even though Daniel was my brother, by now I'd taken on the role of his mum. In fact he now called me 'Mum' and I didn't correct him. As far as he was concerned, I was the nearest he'd ever get to having a mother.

As for Charlie, he believed we were now in a proper, grown-up relationship. Soon after Mum had moved out, he'd told me I now had to sleep in his room every night. All my stuff stayed in my room but at night I was in his bed.

Every day I'd take Daniel to school, come home, get a taxi to school, come back, pick up Daniel, clean up the house, cook dinner and take care of Charlie's sexual needs. My duties too were the same as any other housewife's – apart from the fact that other housewives don't go to school and their husband isn't in fact their stepdad.

At that point Charlie started getting more demanding too. He expected the house to be spotless. Every day, at 5 p.m. on the dot, he'd come back from work then go from room to room to inspect my cleaning. If it wasn't perfect – and I mean not a speck of dust – he'd go mad.

'Get this fucking house tidy!' he'd yell at me.

Then he'd stand there watching as I went over the place again with the vacuum and the duster.

One time we'd gone through this daily routine when Charlie noticed a piece of toffee paper Daniel had dropped on the floor, after I'd vacuumed.

He pushed me onto the settee, slapped me across the face with all his might and shouted, 'What do you call that on the floor? That isn't clean, is it?'

The hitting and beating continued throughout my

pregnancy – but Charlie was always careful to hit me on the arm.

Once he marched me round the house, room to room, pointing out all the spots I'd missed – there was a cup on the floor in the bedroom, I hadn't folded the clothes properly in Daniel's room, dust on the fireplace. It went on and on as he shouted in my face, his strong grip digging into my arm. My arm was black and blue for weeks afterwards.

At night I had to perform my duties with equal care. Charlie refused to accept it if I told him I didn't want sex – he'd scream and shout, calling me every single name under the sun.

'You, fat, lazy bitch!' he'd shout in my face. 'You're fat and ugly. Who do you think would want you? Nobody! Nobody would want you! You're just like your mum!'

That was what hurt the most – I didn't want to be anything like my mum.

Then, he'd force himself on me anyway, putting his hand over my mouth and crushing my bump.

'Now you won't say no to me!' he'd say afterwards.

I'd pick myself up and drag myself to the bathroom where I'd spend another hour washing myself.

I was seven months pregnant when I became subject to a supervision order by the courts. Mum and Charlie were now going through their divorce and from what

I could gather at the time, it was bitter and nasty. Mum hadn't bought into our whole pretence of Alex and had voiced her concerns about the identity of my baby's father to her health visitor.

Added to the school's worries, this meant social services had a sense something wasn't right with me at home.

One morning the social worker Joanna rang Charlie up and told him she was coming to take me out for lunch the next day. Normally, whenever we had any visits, Charlie was always there to make sure I didn't say anything that could land him in trouble.

When Charlie put the phone down that morning he turned to me. 'Joanna's coming to pick you up tomorrow to have a word with you and bring you back,' he said. 'Just remember one thing – say anything and you're dead.'

I honestly believed that was true. I'd become so brainwashed. In my mind there was no way I could reveal the truth to anybody because I thought that once I'd told somebody, I would still have to go home to Charlie and wait for something to happen. And then what? Even if they believed me, even if they eventually came to take me away, I was sure that there would be a time gap between my telling the social worker and being rescued from home – and what would happen in that gap? He'd kill me. I never once thought that I would be taken into protective care – why would I? No one had ever protected me, not even my own mother, so how could I count on strangers?

So when Joanna came to take me out the next day, I was prepared to lie.

We walked to the end of the road to the cafe next to Sainsbury's and she bought me a small Coke and jam and cream scone. After we'd got settled, she leaned in and came right out with it.

'Look, I've got something to ask you. We want to know if Charlie's doing anything to you. Is the baby his?'

I shook my head innocently, plucking crumbs from my plate, careful not to give anything away.

There was a long silence then she sighed and carried on.

'The thing is, Tina, your mum thinks that Charlie is abusing you. She says you don't go out, you don't have friends so she doesn't understand how you could have gone to a party and met a boy you slept with. She thinks that Charlie is the dad.'

This was my opportunity! Of course, I was dying to say, 'Yes, it's true. Please get me away from all this!'

But I couldn't. If I told, there would be consequences for me, consequences she couldn't imagine.

So I just said, 'No, nothing's going on. My mum's lying to you. There's nothing going on.'

Inside I felt my heart beating madly but I tried to steady my nerves. I wanted so much for the truth to come out but how could I tell her? How could I tell anyone and live to see another day?

She dropped me back off later and told Charlie: 'Right, I'll be back in touch.'

Four days later a letter landed on the mat – it was from the courts requesting a DNA test on the baby when he was born to prove the paternity.

I read the letter after Charlie put it down. I didn't really know what it meant. All I saw were the words 'blood test' – I didn't realise the implications.

But Charlie knew. And two months later we unexpectedly moved twenty miles away to a whole different county.

Chapter 6
Changes

A week after Christmas 1995 Charlie announced we were moving. He didn't say why, and I didn't ask. I had an idea by now it was something to do with the baby and social services finding out who the father was, but I didn't question Charlie. I'd learned not to.

He drove us to the town that would be our new home that day to look at the new place and at first we got horribly lost, driving round and round these little back streets in the dark, looking for our new house.

When we finally found it, I was pleased to see it had a really big garden – I loved going outside and sitting in the garden, doing nothing, just loving the peace and quiet and the chance to be on my own for a few short moments. Charlie just stamped around the place with the estate agent following behind, inspecting every room as I sat in the living room with Daniel. Finally he nodded: 'Okay, let's go.'

It obviously met with his approval because a couple of weeks later we packed up and moved.

At the beginning of my pregnancy, when I could fantasise that the father of my baby was the perfect, imaginary Alex, I looked forward to having a little baby on my own.

But as much as I wanted the fantasy to be real, it wasn't. As my bump grew larger and larger, Charlie, oddly, became more and more proud of becoming a father again, while I lost interest in my baby. My emotions were much too raw, too scary to be acknowledged, and so I locked them away inside myself. It was better to be numb. I'd been through so much pain already in my life that if I stopped for a moment to feel it, I'd probably never stop crying. Most times, I was just a shell.

Other expectant mums loved going shopping for their soon-to-be borns; I had lost interest. I remember going along with Charlie to Mothercare just before the baby arrived. There was Charlie, walking around the shop, picking out outfits and buying all the baby equipment we needed, but I just stood in the background, not really caring about what he bought.

Just below the numbness was a new emotion that I struggled hard to suppress. I was terrified of the baby being born and looking like Charlie. I felt panic whenever I thought of it. Soon a child was going to arrive, the product of Charlie's abuse. It wasn't the baby's fault, but still, I had lost that feeling of joy I felt when I first found out I was pregnant.

Two weeks after we arrived in our new home, I started at a new mother-and-baby unit while Charlie landed a job as a taxi driver. There were six of us in my new class in a great big building and this time, we only had one subject – childcare. No more art, no more cookery or swimming, just six girls and a handful of babies. There was just one classroom and a small room on the landing where we had the crèche. In the morning two of us would look after the babies in the crèche while the other four studied childcare, and then after lunch we'd swap round.

By now I was eight and a half months pregnant, enormous and running out of energy – it was harder than ever to go to school, look after Daniel and make sure the house was clean and tidy. Still, I was scared of what was to come. Back at my old mother-and-baby unit, most of the girls had already had their babies and they'd come back to school, full of horror stories about long, painful labours.

One girl had been in labour for two days. When I asked her what it felt like, she thought for a bit then answered: 'Well, you know period pains?'

I nodded.

'It's like a thousand times worse than that!'

Oh my god, I nearly peed myself with fear!

I didn't have to wait long to find out for myself – three weeks after I started at the new mother-and-baby unit, I went into labour.

My blood pressure had shot up in the last few weeks of the pregnancy and the doctors were concerned

I might have pre-eclampsia so they took me into the local hospital to be induced.

They gave me a pessary and made me lie on the bed for half an hour with strict instructions not to move – but the pessary brought on the contractions almost immediately and I lay there, in agony, desperately trying not to move as the pain swept over my body in waves.

'*She was right,*' I thought to myself, gasping as the contractions built. It's really bad! At least a thousand times worse than period pains! But as I groaned and squirmed, Charlie sat in the chair next to my bed, shooting dirty looks in my direction.

'Oh, shut up!' he barked when the pains were so bad I screamed. 'It's not that bad!'

By now they'd strapped me up to a baby monitor, which showed that every time I had a contraction the baby's heart rate dropped. The midwife seemed concerned and went away to get the doctor.

'What does it mean?' I asked Charlie, between contractions. I was so young, so scared and all this was new. 'Is the baby all right?'

But he just shrugged.

Two minutes later the doctor came in and watched the monitor as I gasped and groaned through another contraction.

She turned to me. 'Look, Tina, we're worried about the baby. It's not doing well so we're going to have to do an emergency Caesarean. Do you understand what that means?'

I nodded, full of fear.

From that moment, I seemed to be surrounded by people – Charlie was bundled out as they inserted a catheter into me then they wheeled me down to theatre. Still lying flat on my back, I tried to look around at all the people in the room. I could see a woman out of the corner of my eye, holding a metal contraption, ready to put down my throat. I was petrified. Oh god, I prayed silently, please let me survive!

Then a mask was held over my face and the next minute, I was gone.

As they were wheeling me into recovery I woke up in terrible pain and to a horrific sight – my gown and bed were soaked in blood. It was everywhere! I wondered for a moment if I'd died, then I lost consciousness again and the next thing I knew I was lying in the maternity ward, all cleaned up and there was a little baby in the cot beside me.

I looked down at the tiny body swaddled in a white blanket and for a moment, I was confused. '*Who is this baby?*' I wondered. Then I remembered – he was *my* baby. But I didn't feel anything.

I hadn't worried too much about not feeling bonded to my child while I was pregnant as I thought

I would be overwhelmed with love for my little boy the moment he was born. But staring at this tiny child next to me, I didn't feel a thing. It didn't even feel like he was mine. One minute I was pregnant, the next I'd woken up from a sleep and there was a baby. And I was in pain – real pain.

After a while, the midwife came in. She bent over the cot and cooed at the tiny baby. 'What a sweet wee thing,' she said, 'I'll always love that new baby smell.'

She picked him up and cradled him in her arms, looking down at my new son with affection written all over her face. 'Have you thought of a name yet?' she asked.

'Alex,' I croaked. Even though there was no way that my pretend boyfriend could have been my son's dad, I wanted to hang on to just a small part of that fantasy. I had run the name past Charlie and he approved, though he didn't understand the reasons why.

The midwife jigged the little baby up and down and Alex made soft gurgling noises. It seemed that she was feeling more love for this newborn than his own mother. I just felt numb.

And then the midwife said, 'Doesn't he look like his grandfather?' and numbness was replaced by a surge of fear. They believed Charlie was my real dad. What was going to happen now? Would the truth come out? Fear prickled all over my skin and gripped my stomach. Fear not just for everything coming out into the open, but also about the future, and how my life was going to change with a new baby. And fear because having Charlie's baby bonded me to him for ever. Was I ever going to be able to get away? Or would my only escape be, as Charlie had told me time and time again, in death?

The midwife's voice broke through my thoughts. 'I think little Alex is hungry. Would you like to try to feed him?'

I nodded. So, she sat me up and placed Alex on my chest but the weight of him on my scar was excruciating and I cried out.

'Too soon?' the midwife said kindly. 'Never mind, I'll just fix him a bottle.'

And off she went, leaving me alone with a small and vulnerable baby. How could I look after him? I was only a child myself.

The first 48 hours of motherhood were terrible – I couldn't even hold Alex properly because of the pain and every time I coughed, I had to hold my scar, frightened that the stitches would burst. I was also drifting in and out of consciousness from the morphine I was given. Nothing seemed quite real. I remember waking up and seeing Charlie cradling Alex in his arms and then drifting off to sleep again.

I wanted to love my little boy but from the very start, I felt absolutely nothing for him. Maybe it was the Caesarean, maybe it was just me, but mostly I think it was because he was the spitting image of Charlie from the top of his soft head to the tips of his tiny toes. Even the midwives remarked on how much he looked like his granddad. So how could I love my little boy?

I was in hospital for four days in total and I spent most of my time crying my eyes out.

'It's the baby blues,' the nurses tried to reassure me. 'Everybody gets them after having a baby.'

If only they knew the truth!

Back home, Charlie swapped from playing the doting grandfather to the doting dad while I became more and more upset. Only now do I know that I was suffering from post-natal depression but back then I had no idea what was wrong with me.

When Charlie was at work, I was left alone with Alex and I went through the motions of motherhood like a robot. If he cried, I fed him. When he was dirty, I washed him and when he soiled himself, I changed him.

But I didn't love him – there was no emotional bond there at all.

Worse, Charlie became even more controlling. No one came to visit me, not even my mum who knew where our new house was, nor any of the other mums at the mother-and-baby unit, so I was utterly alone, and Charlie knew that too. He knew that he could do what- ever he liked to me, have sex with me whenever he wanted, hit me, yell at me, and nothing would happen. Where would I go? I was still only fifteen years old and had no one. No one except for Charlie.

When most girls my age were out having fun, going to see bands, meeting new people and discovering the world, my world became ever more regimented and narrow. In the mornings Charlie would get up before me and lay out the clothes he wanted Alex to wear – I wasn't allowed to choose. If I got up earlier than him and put him into a romper suit that I liked, Charlie would undress him and then throw the clothes he'd chosen in my face. 'Put them on him, now!'

So then I had to redress him in what Charlie wanted.

I was still meant to carry out my cleaning duties but now I wasn't allowed to vacuum if Alex was asleep, in case it woke him up.

And if I went to pick him up for a feed, Charlie would shout at me, 'Leave him be. He's sleeping!' So my relations with my son were strictly controlled and it made everything worse.

Two weeks later I was back at the mother-and-baby unit, studying childcare again.

It was deadly dull but at least I wasn't at home, staring at the four walls, waiting for the clock to hit 5 p.m. when Charlie would come in.

The one good thing about the unit was that we could come and go as we pleased. One afternoon the taxi was late picking us up so I walked to the shops with another girl to get a drink. Just my luck, that very afternoon Charlie decided to ring the unit.

'What do you mean, she's not there?' he shouted down the phone to my teacher. 'I'm going to kill her when she gets in!'

When I got back to the unit, the teacher told me my dad had been in touch and he seemed really angry. '*Oh no*,' I thought wearily. Now I didn't want to go home at all but I knew I had to go back and face the music.

Charlie was standing outside the front of the house when the taxi pulled up, his face a picture of rage.

I dragged myself in the front door, my legs heavy and leaden, while he stomped in after me before slamming it shut.

'Where were you?' he demanded. 'Why didn't you come home when you were meant to come home?'

I tried to explain the taxi had been late and I went to the shops to get a drink but he wasn't having any of it.

One minute I was talking, the next I felt an almighty thwack across my face.

'You're full of shit!' he screamed at the top of his voice. 'What have you been up to? Who have you been speaking to? You been out talking to boys?'

I couldn't get my words out, I was shaking and crying with fear and misery. I just wanted it all to stop but he kept going, on and on and on. Eventually I slunk upstairs to bed and wrapped myself in the duvet, still sobbing. He didn't care of course – as long as he got sex that night he was happy.

I must have cried myself to sleep because the next thing I knew, he was rolling me onto my back and lowering himself onto me. I just lay there with my eyes closed, tears trickling down my face, as he put his penis inside me and did what he wanted.

After that I pulled myself out of bed and went to the bathroom, as usual, to wash myself.

'There she bloody goes!' he called out after me. 'Always off to the bathroom. What do you have to do that for, you stupid bitch?'

He couldn't understand why I did it – I suppose by now he thought that I wanted to have sex with him. He really had no idea how much I hated it and I didn't explain. The fact was, it didn't make me feel any better but it did make me feel a bit cleaner.

Clean and rid of him. It was the only thing I could do, within this cage of fear that I was living, to make me feel vaguely human.

By now I felt like a zombie. I had to have sex with Charlie because I didn't have any choice. It was a question of doing it or suffer a beating. So of course I did it.

Even after sex, he made me play with him until he fell asleep. If I fell asleep first, he'd nudge me awake and make me play with him until he was fast asleep. Only then was I allowed to sleep.

I tried to block it out. While he was on top of me, I would escape into my own imaginary world, a place where I was having a good time and a good life.

I'd picture myself walking through a sunlit field of flowers, my hair blowing in the wind, the grass skimming my knees. Or splashing along a beach, playing ball with my brother and sister, laughing and having fun. In my mind, I could make it all go away – even if it was only for a short while.

Charlie's angry threats on the phone to my teacher made them worry about me at home and since I was still on a supervision order, social services came round a couple of times to see me.

But they didn't know what was really going on – I think they were just told to check up and report back to the social services in our old town. The health visitor came and I told all the usual lies and because we'd now moved to a different county, the DNA test never happened. So after a few months the order expired and we were left alone again.

As I saw it, social services were never going to help me. No one was. If I was ever going to escape, it would have been back, before I got pregnant. But now, with a baby, I was more imprisoned than ever. If it had been next to impossible to escape from Charlie's clutches before Alex came along, it was out of the question now.

Six months after Alex was born, Mum and I had a massive row on the phone. I was fed up – we had barely spoken since my son arrived, she hadn't come to see her new grandchild, and all she was saying to me was the usual – that she hated me, that she had never loved me, that she wished I was dead.

And for the first time I answered her back: 'Yeah? Well, you know what? I wish you were dead too!'

Those were the last words I ever spoke to her.

The next day a call came through at home while Charlie was at work. It was my nana – Mum's mum. I hadn't spoken to her in months but she didn't seem to want to talk to me.

'Where's Charlie? Is Charlie in?' she asked. Her voice sounded strained and I just knew something wasn't right.

'No, he's at work,' I said. 'Why? What's wrong?'

'I need to speak to Charlie as soon as possible,' was all she'd say. 'Get him to ring me when he gets in.'

At that moment I heard my granddad shouting in the background: 'For fuck's sake – just tell her!'

I was scared by now. 'Right, come on!' I said. 'What's wrong?'

Nana sighed. 'Your mum's dead,' she said simply, then hung up.

For the next minute, I just stood there with the phone still in my hand and the dead tone ringing in my ear, not really comprehending what she'd just said.

Then, as I carefully replaced the receiver, a big sob welled up inside me and I collapsed on the floor in tears. I told Charlie when he came home and he said, 'Oh right, okay.' He didn't really care. He had no feelings for my mum.

Later on, I found out she'd had an epileptic fit and her brother had found her dead in the house when he went round to see her that morning.

Charlie took me to the funeral a week later, but we didn't take Daniel and Alex as they were too young. There I saw my brother and sister for the first time in months – they were with their new foster carer Kathleen – and I was pleased to see they looked clean and well cared for.

I felt very awkward and uncomfortable – there were loads of people there I didn't know – and nobody seemed to know who I was either.

During the service my nana and granddad sat in the front row while us kids sat at the very back. At the very end the priest mentioned all of mum's brothers and sisters, her parents and even Charlie – but he didn't say a word about me, Lisa, Paul or Daniel.

The three of us held a single red rose each and later, after everyone had left the church, I approached the front with our flowers. The coffin had disappeared behind a curtain, ready for the cremation.

'Excuse me,' I shyly addressed the priest. 'Could you put these on top of the coffin for me please?'

'You can put them on top of the coffin yourself if you want,' he said then he pulled the curtain back a bit to allow me to put the roses on top.

In the doorway I could see my nana and granddad, talking to Lisa and Paul, but I just ignored them.

I went up to the coffin and put my hand on top of the cold smooth wood. I couldn't believe my mum was dead inside that large box. Then I placed the roses on top with my other hand and leant against the casket, my cheek now touching the wood.

'I'm sorry, Mum,' I whispered, tears stinging my eyes. 'I didn't mean what I said.'

I just stood there, holding the coffin and letting the tears fall until Charlie pulled me away and I walked out.

Just then, the priest took Charlie aside. 'Who is she?' he asked, pointing at me.

'That's her daughter,' Charlie replied, nodding to the casket.

'Oh dear!' the priest was suddenly running after me. 'I'm so sorry. I'm truly very sorry. I didn't realise! Nobody told me she had children. If I'd known I would have sat you at the front.'

'It doesn't matter,' I said, before walking out. 'It really doesn't matter.'

After the initial shock of her death, and the guilt at feeling I was in some way responsible, I was left with a strange mix of emotions. I'd stopped loving my mum years ago so I couldn't pretend that her death affected me greatly but I was sad at how everything had turned out.

Sad for her, sad for me, and for Lisa, Daniel and Paul.

I vowed I was never going to give my kids the same life that she gave me. I vowed I'd never follow in her footsteps.

I'd always put my kids first and I'd always be there for them.

Chapter 7
Housebound

The lights blinked mechanically on the tree as the sunlight streamed through the window of Charlie's mum's house, where we were sat having our Christmas dinner, my first as a mum.

'Come on,' Charlie nudged me. 'Snap out of it – it's bloody Christmas!'

I gave him a faint smile but inside, I was a world away.

Charlie's mum had these beautiful little glass figurines on her mantelpiece which, when they caught the light, projected a rainbow of colours over the walls. I was lost in those colours, my mind wandering over the points of light as they danced and swirled different patterns on the walls.

Christmas didn't mean a damn thing to me any more.

A few weeks before Charlie had bought a Christmas tree and given me twenty pounds to get some shopping. I'd spotted a little ornament in a shop, which I thought was cute. It was a small plaster shoe with the words: 'Baby's First Christmas.'

When I got home I hung it on our tree but when Charlie came in from work he ripped it off the tree then stamped on it until it broke into tiny white shards. I was ordered to clear it up.

I wasn't allowed to choose anything any more. Not even a single Christmas ornament.

Alex's birth had been accompanied by the realisation that if I'd felt trapped before, there was no getting out of my situation now. The door had slammed shut. I couldn't leave a child. And as the months went on, and Charlie's control over me tightened, my depression took me to frightening new depths.

Those tiny moments of escape were all I had. The rainbows dancing on the walls.

Charlie's temper was worse than ever.

One lunchtime I was in the kitchen, heating up a jar of spaghetti bolognese in the bottle warmer for Alex when Charlie came in.

'What are you doing?'

'I'm feeding him.'

He plucked the jar out of the bottle warmer, examined it carefully then said, 'Who said you can give him this?'

'Nobody.'

His face darkened and the next second, he hurled it at the wall.

There was a frightening smash as glass and spaghetti bolognese flew everywhere and the sauce splattered down the kitchen wall.

Then he walked calmly to the cupboard, got out a jar of cottage pie and handed it to me. 'Here you go – feed him that.'

Charlie had chosen all the flavours anyway so it wasn't that he disapproved of the food – he just objected to the fact that I hadn't asked him first.

Shaking with fear, I went to put the jar in the warmer, but Charlie hadn't finished with me yet. As he was walking out the door, he said, 'Before you feed him, clean that mess up.'

So I was on my hands and knees clearing up all the glass and spaghetti before I could feed Alex. After-wards I set about cleaning the reddish-brown stain off the walls.

Half an hour later I was still at it when Charlie came back in. He took one look at the faded pink stain and slapped me across the face. 'When I get home from work, I want that stain off the wall!'

I tried, I really did but it was hopeless. I spent hours trying to get that stain off but nothing worked – I tried bleach, washing up liquid, even washing powder! But that stain refused to budge and in the end Charlie painted over the whole wall.

*

By now I was no longer at the mother-and-baby unit – I'd stayed there three months after Alex was born before finally getting sick of studying nothing but childcare. And I still hadn't bonded with my baby. I felt disconnected from him, and it was difficult seeing the other young mums with their babies and how much they loved them. I felt nothing.

'I'm not going back there,' I told Charlie one morning.

He just shrugged his shoulders – it didn't matter to him. But I didn't want to be stuck in the house all day either so I looked into going to college. I found a foundation course for Accountancy at the local college which I might qualify for if I passed the entrance test.

I nervously asked Charlie if I could go and he said he'd think about it. A few days later he gave me his response. 'All right, you can do it, but on one condition, I drop you off and pick you up.'

I readily agreed and set about preparing for the exam – I'd always been good at maths in school, even though I hadn't studied it for a while, so accountancy felt right for me. As the months passed, I waited anxiously for the results.

In the meantime my life became confined entirely to our house.

I wasn't even allowed to have a key so when Charlie left, I was stuck at home with Alex all day long. The only time I got to go out was to drop Daniel off at school and pick him up again. Charlie was always at home when I did this so he'd leave the back door open for me to get in again. Then of an evening, Charlie would take us shopping at the supermarket. And when we were out together, I had to walk behind him.

The fact was, I was getting older and that's why Charlie had to ratchet up the control. When you're a small child, threats are enough to keep you in line, but threats don't have the same power after a while. Now that I was fifteen and a half, Charlie had to step up the control and the violence so that I was constantly in fear.

I'd opened a bank account back in March so I could start getting benefits for Alex but Charlie had made me put his name on the account and he kept all the cards, so I had no access to money at all. When we went to the shops, he came with me and he always paid.

If he asked me to go to the shop down the road, he'd give me a precise list of what he wanted and I'd have to bring him back the items, the change and the receipt and stand there waiting while he added it all up, just to check I hadn't stolen any money off him.

One time he asked me to go to the shop and gave me a ten-pound note.

'I want Coke, bread, milk and cat food,' he said. 'Go now and don't be long.'

I went to the shop and paid for it all then brought back the shopping, the change and the receipt for him as usual. This time he was a penny short and he started screaming and shouting at me – where's the penny? Why was I stealing from him?

I'd obviously been short-changed but Charlie refused to accept this. In the end I told him I bought a penny sweet, just to shut him up.

If I needed new clothes, Charlie would go out and buy them for me or he'd take me to the market where he'd decide what I could wear. Usually it was big baggy T-shirts and men's trousers because they were the only clothes that fitted me. By now I was nearly twenty stone. I'd put on loads of weight from comfort eating and when I was out, I felt fat and self-conscious. Charlie told me often enough I was fat and ugly and when I looked at myself in the mirror I'd think: 'Yeah, he's right. I am horrible.'

It was another means of control, I believe. By taking away all my rights – the right to choose the clothes I wore, the right to leave my own house when I wanted, the right to say no to his constant sexual abuse – I had become a prisoner inside my own mind. Charlie telling me that I was fat and ugly just reinforced the idea that my mum had put inside my head since I was little: that I was worthless and that there was no one out there who'd ever want me. Apart, that is, from my prison guard, Charlie.

During the day, I'd cook, clean, tidy and wash up then watch *Neighbours*, *Home and Away* and *Murder She Wrote*.

I liked that programme – it gave me some good ideas about how I could kill Charlie. One episode showed a man who was poisoned but when they did an autopsy, they couldn't find the drug that had poisoned him. It had been absorbed into his system.

'*That's what I need*,' I thought. '*A drug they can't detect to kill him!*'

Of course, I'd never seriously do something like that, but I liked to dream of being free of Charlie, no matter how sinister those dreams were.

Ever since the thumb incident, Charlie had pampered Daniel and spoilt him rotten.

One evening I'd just given Daniel his tea of sausage, beans and chips and he tipped up his plate and it went all over the floor.

'Pick that up!' I demanded. 'I've just made that for you.'

But Charlie wasn't having any of it.

'He doesn't have to pick it up – *you* pick it up.'

I stood there for a few seconds, frustration and humiliation welling up inside me, desperate to defy him and run out of that house. Even if I wasn't locked in, I didn't have anywhere to go! And not to mention there was no money to run away with. But my deeper fear was that Charlie would find me and kill me. I could not see that I had any other options

'I said do it!' Charlie growled at me from the settee. 'Don't make me come over there!'

Fear made me drop to my knees. I didn't want to risk yet another beating.

So there I was, crawling around the floor. I had no choice. Like with everything else in my life, it was either do it, or get beaten. And I did everything I could to avoid a beating.

On top of all this my life had become a pack of lies.

From the moment we'd moved here, Charlie had started to introduce me as his partner to all our neighbours, and Charlie's work colleagues thought I was his girlfriend, not his stepdaughter. He obviously told them I was older than fifteen but I had no idea what age he'd given me so I was always wary when the neighbours talked to me in case I said the wrong thing and got into trouble.

Of course this made for some difficult situations – one of the girls from my mother-and-baby unit lived across the street and she knew Charlie as my dad.

So I had to make sure I wasn't with any of the other neighbours when she was around. The doctors and health visitors all knew Charlie as my dad too so my mind was in a constant spin, trying to make sure I was telling the right story to the right person.

I nearly slipped up once at the doctor's when I started crying from the depression.

'What's wrong, Miss Jenkins?' the doctor asked kindly.

'It's Charlie... I mean... it's my dad. He's been shouting at me and I can't take it no more.'

A couple of days later they sent a health visitor to check up on me, now concerned for my well-being.

'I've come to have a word with Tina,' said the health visitor when she arrived out of the blue one morning.

'Yeah, that's fine,' said Charlie. 'I'm going to work anyway.'

And he marched out of the house, making a big show of slamming the door behind him.

She sat down in the living room and we went through the usual rigmarole of her asking me how I was getting on at home.

'Yeah, fine,' I replied, knowing not to give anything away

'The doctor said you'd been in and you were upset.'

'I just got down that day – my dad had been shouting at me.'

This went on for some minutes before she left – all the while Charlie had sneaked in the back door and was listening from the kitchen. I never knew until I read the health visitor's notes years later – she knew he was still there, listening to us.

Charlie didn't waste any time – he changed doctors and that was that. We had a new doctor and a new health visitor and no one was any wiser. That was his strategy for dealing with any tricky situation – the moment anyone got suspicious, he'd make a change and the problem would go away.

But my depression didn't go away. Before Alex was born I still had the fantasy in my head of living the perfect life with my little baby. But from the moment he arrived, my life just seemed to get worse and worse.

We'd moved, I had no family around, my mum was dead and I never saw Lisa and Paul. I didn't go out, I didn't have friends and I lived a life of slavery to Charlie's demands and sexual whims. Now I was totally alone and there was no escaping.

My daydreams turned to thoughts of killing myself. When we were out shopping, I'd watch the cars go past and imagine walking in front of one. Or I could top myself with drugs, or drink bleach, overdose on painkillers, slit my wrists, jump out of a window… the list went on and on.

One day we were in Charlie's car, driving down the motorway to his mother's, when this fantasy reared up in my head. I pictured grabbing the steering wheel and pulling on it sharply, so that the car would head into oncoming traffic. I could wait until a large lorry was coming the other way. I imagined the crash and pictured myself flying through the window and landing like a broken doll on the road. Or perhaps the whole car would go up in a ball of flames? That way I would be gone, but Charlie would be gone too – I could take him with me. I smiled a little to myself then. He couldn't control my thoughts, he didn't know that I wanted him dead.

The impulse to carry out my fantasy was strong, very strong, almost overwhelming. But then I heard a little gurgling laugh in the back seat. Alex was being tickled by his big brother Daniel. Seeing them together meant that I couldn't go through with it.

I may not have felt a mother's love for Alex, but I did bring him into the world and had a responsibility to him. I realised then that I couldn't abandon him, not by walking out of the house and certainly not in death.

Me and my poor little boy were both trapped in this hell.

Then, in the August, I got the first piece of good news I'd had in a long time – I'd passed the test to get into college! I was due to start the following month. That little bit of paper meant so much to me and at nights I started to dream again of a life outside of Charlie's sick and violent world. I'd pass my accountancy exams, I'd get a job and I'd earn enough money to secure a future for myself and Alex. '*One day we'd escape this place,*' I dared to dream, '*one day.*'

Chapter 8
College

On my first day of college I was nervous as hell. Charlie drove me to the gates and glowered at me as I slipped out of his car.

'Just don't go talking to any boys!' he warned.

'No, I won't,' I said. And honestly, I didn't want to. I'd never properly been among boys before so the thought of talking to one scared me half to death.

Walking into that large building full of young, slim and good-looking girls and boys was absolutely terrifying. '*So this is what normal teenagers looked like,*' I thought. They seemed so cool, relaxed, happy and at ease with themselves. Boys were everywhere – chatting in groups, backpacks slung casually on their shoulders, smoking outside, wearing trendy clothes and the girls standing next to them were sleek and well groomed.

I felt like a dollop of lard compared to these gorgeous creatures so I just kept my head down and headed for the classroom for my first lesson.

For years all I'd ever known was girls' schools and then the mother-and-baby units. I'd never really been in an environment with boys in and it seemed so alien.

117

Between lessons I'd walk past them in the corridors and pray they weren't looking at me. If they were standing talking in a corner I'd imagine they were looking at me and talking about me – I was shy and intimidated.

My heart used to beat faster every time a group of boys came in or walked past. I'd just keep my head down or pretend I was looking for something in my bag when I wasn't. That became quite a regular thing – looking for things in my bag!

Sometimes I'd have to take Alex in with me – he was just six months old so I'd carry him in his car seat and he'd sleep under the desk during lessons. Before I started college I had asked the teachers if I could bring him in occasionally, and they were fine with it – I wasn't the only teenage mum there. Besides, Alex was no trouble at all, and everyone commented on how cute he was. I was always relieved when I had Alex – it gave me something else to think about instead of all the people chattering around me.

Charlie told me that I wasn't allowed to go and sit in the canteen at mealtimes – he thought this was too dangerous. If I actually made friends, then I might let something slip, and he couldn't have that. Instead he'd meet me at the gates in his car and I'd sit there for an hour. I didn't mind – it saved me the embarrassment of sitting in the canteen on my own.

The lessons weren't so bad, except I found it hard to concentrate when there were so many boys around.

Plus, I'd never taken my GCSEs so I didn't have the experience of studying properly. I was probably the only person in that college without a single GCSE to my name. And I refused to answer any questions or put my hand up in class.

It had been the same at school – I was so shy and self-conscious I never opened my mouth, not even to ask for help. So if I didn't understand something there wasn't much I could do about it. At school I'd managed to study German for two whole years without once speaking the language in class. At the end of every lesson our teacher would go round the class asking everyone a question in German, which you had to answer before you could leave.

I was always the last person left in the class after everyone had gone because I refused to speak. After a while the teacher would sigh and give in. 'Okay, you can go now Tina.'

It was the same for all the other lessons, except drama. I hated drama so much I'd skip that lesson and hide in the toilets. Talking in front of people? Acting in front of them? No way. It wasn't going to happen. Charlie's spirit had snaked around my neck, stopped me from speaking, his hands were over my eyes, making me avoid eye contact. And his words were constantly in my ears, telling me that I was worthless, fat and ugly, and drowning out other people's attempts to help me.

In college it was the same, I simply couldn't focus because I already had so much going on in my head, I always had *Charlie* in my head. To me, the stuff going on in class wasn't important. It wasn't relevant. Surviving at home, now that was important.

I tried my best to concentrate on the lessons but I also had to think about how to avoid speaking to people to stop me getting into trouble with Charlie.

And I didn't have time to do homework. I'd have to go home, cook, clean, wash the clothes and make the house spotless and if it wasn't, I had to do it over again and over again until it was perfect.

One night after class, I was still cleaning at midnight. God knows why Charlie wanted the place so clean – nobody ever came to the house! Still, at least college meant I could escape Charlie for a few hours a day and even if I wasn't doing brilliantly I was trying my best and gradually I started to get to grips with accountancy.

That December Charlie took me to his work's Christmas do. By now I was sixteen, though Charlie told everyone I was in my twenties. It was held in a large hall and each long table was taken up by a local business. Of course, he hadn't asked me if I wanted to go – he arranged for his mum to babysit Alex and Daniel and that was that. I didn't question him, I hardly ever did any more.

Malik, Charlie's boss, owned three businesses in the area so all the staff and their partners were on the same table together while on other tables there were solicitors, accountants and greengrocers.

As I walked in I was struck by the excitement in the air – people running from table to table, kissing each other, clinking glasses and chatting excitedly. Charlie too was in a party mood, introducing me to everyone as his partner, seemingly proud to have me at his side. But every time he smiled in my direction, I shrank back into my seat. I couldn't even pretend to be proud of Charlie.

I smiled at every new person I met but on the whole, kept my mouth shut. I didn't know what to say – I was still a teenager and I'd never been out to a party before, mixing with adults.

I hadn't known what to wear either so I'd put on black suit trousers, a white blouse and a black jacket – I looked like I was going to a funeral! 'Smile, for God's sake!' Charlie whispered, as I nursed my Coke and sneaked furtive peeks at all the sophisticated women, clicking across the dance floor in their high heels and party frocks.

But how could I? I didn't know what to say to people! So I just sat there, watching all the other people at the tables get drunk, laugh and dance about.

A disco ball twirled in the middle of the dance floor, sending out rays of light onto the tables and walls – and for a long time I just stared at that, transfixed by the spinning lights, withdrawing again into my own world.

When our dinner came, it gave me a good excuse not to talk to anybody but the food wasn't up to much. The starter was this thick green vegetable soup which looked like someone had puked into a bowl. The main was slightly better – steak with potatoes and a peppercorn sauce. And afterwards there was a choice of ice cream or orange sorbet. I stuck with the ice cream, twirling the spoon round in my bowl and watching Charlie get more and more drunk as the night wore on.

He was having a great old time – laughing, chatting and charming the pants off everyone. People seemed to like Charlie and I knew why – he put on an act. When he wanted to, he could turn on the charm the way he switched on the anger when he was back at home.

Everyone thought he was the bee's knees.

All of a sudden, Malik was standing at our table, one hand holding a glass of red wine, his other arm clutching a young, good-looking boy around my age.

'Everyone!' he announced proudly. 'This is my son, Maz. He's following me into the family businesses. You should all get to know him because one day he'll be taking over from me!'

People nodded or stood to shake his hand, but I just kept swirling my ice cream round in my bowl. Eventually Malik turned and introduced me and Charlie to

Maz and Charlie shook his hand – I didn't speak. I knew Charlie wouldn't have wanted me to talk to a boy my age so I didn't. I just gave him one of my half-hearted smiles then turned away, waiting for the moment we could leave so I could stop worrying about how awful I must have looked to everyone else.

By May I was just beginning to find my feet at college when I walked into the library one morning and saw Maz, talking to his friends.

I was so shocked I ran and hid round the corner.

My heart was racing wildly and I could barely catch my breath. What if he saw me? What if he wanted to come over and talk to me – then what would I say?

I was meant to be Charlie's partner, probably somewhere in my twenties, so how could I explain being in college?

My head was spinning for the rest of the day and that night I told Charlie I'd seen Maz.

'What do you mean? He can't be there – he's away studying down south. You're wrong.'

But the next day I saw Maz again, standing in the corridor with a big group of boys and girls.

This time he spotted me and shouted out: 'Hi, Tina!'

I was like a rabbit caught in the headlights. There was no way I could go over and talk to him – so once again, I ran off.

And that night I told Charlie I wasn't mistaken, Maz was definitely going to my college.

Over the next few days, Charlie managed to find out Maz had got a transfer to my college so that was it – he pulled me out of college.

My dream of taking Alex and starting a life away from Charlie was over. I'm sure that most people would have felt upset about that, but I didn't even cry. The thing was – I was relieved that I wouldn't have to explain to anyone why I was in college when I was supposed to be too old for that. That's how brainwashed I was – I cared less about my future plans than I did about upsetting Charlie. He had wormed his way into my mind so much that I was losing all sense of self-preservation.

Surprisingly – and inconsistently, given that he wanted me to be under his control twenty-four hours a day – a couple of weeks after I finished college, Charlie enrolled me for driving lessons. He'd managed to get a deal with a company run by a husband-and-wife team for eighteen pounds a lesson and once a week, after Charlie finished work, I was picked up at 6 p.m. for an hour's driving lesson by the wife.

Being with a woman made me comfortable though on those first few lessons, I was dead nervous.

One week, she took me out on a Sunday and we drove to a deserted industrial estate near our house.

'Right,' she said. 'Today you're going to learn how to do an emergency stop. You'll need to drive at thirty miles an hour and then when I put my hand up you've got to brake hard. Got it?'

I nodded.

'Okay, then start.'

So I started driving, slowly at first, just ten miles an hour.

And out of the corner of my eye I was watching my instructor, waiting for her to put her hand up.

'Come on, speed up a bit,' she said.

So I pressed on the accelerator a bit harder and got up to fifteen miles an hour.

I was still looking at her, watching, waiting for her hand to go up, but she just sat there, her hands folded neatly in her lap.

Very, very slowly I started to go faster, first to twenty then thirty miles an hour.

Suddenly she lifted her hand and I slammed on the brakes with all my strength.

We stopped dead.

'That was really, really good,' she smiled at me. 'But why did it take you so long to get up to speed?'

I couldn't answer her – except I knew why. I was always used to anticipating Charlie's every move, so it came naturally to me to keep checking to see what she was doing.

I came to love my driving lessons. It was an hour of freedom once a week without Charlie, and thoughts of escape seemed to creep into my mind – if I could learn to drive then maybe one day I'd be able to get away from him.

My instructor was encouraging and supportive and over time, I got my head around the mechanics of driving. But then one day, my instructor was ill and her husband came to pick me up for my driving lesson instead.

Charlie scowled as I got into the car with him that evening and I knew I'd be in trouble when I got home. Sure enough, as soon as the lesson was over and I walked back into the house, he laid into me.

'What did you say to him?'

'Nothing. We just talked about driving.'

'Liar! You were flirting with him! You were chatting him up!'

Flirting? I didn't even know how to flirt! The accusations went on all night and something told me my driving lessons were about to come to a swift end.

The next morning, my fears were confirmed.

'You're not doing that driving any more,' Charlie said over breakfast. 'You'll have to call them up – tell them you'll be stopping.'

I was prepared for it, but still, I couldn't help a lump rising in my throat. Charlie wasn't just jealous, he treated me as his property. He could tell me to do something, then change his mind, and it would all be okay because I wasn't allowed even the slightest bit of control over my life. As far as Charlie was concerned, I was his, to do what he wanted with. And I was so beaten down that I couldn't stand up to him, I just couldn't.

So as soon as I'd finished my toast, cleared away the plates and washed up, I got on the phone.

'I can't do the lessons any more,' I said.

'Oh, that's a shame,' he replied. 'May I ask why?'

I thought on my feet. 'Erm, we can't afford it,' I said. 'We haven't got the money at the moment. I'll start again when we've got the money to spare.'

He accepted that and rang off.

'Anyway,' said Charlie, pulling on his jacket for work. 'You don't need an instructor any more. You've had enough lessons – I'll take you out.'

But Charlie's driving lessons turned out to be a disaster. Unlike the kindly woman who gave me soft words of encouragement, Charlie barked orders and shouted commands like a sergeant major.

'You're too close to the kerb!' he'd scream, making me jump and swerve in the road.

The longer the lesson went on, the more Charlie shouted and the more nervous I became, making silly mistakes I'd never normally make.

Finally, on our way back home, we approached a tiny roundabout where Charlie told me to take the third turning.

Now in my lessons I was used to driving a small Fiat Punto but Charlie took me out in his large Ford Mondeo – it was like driving a tank! And unlike the Punto, it was too big to go round the roundabout properly.

But I didn't know this at the time so I made to go round the roundabout as usual and Charlie started shouting at me. 'What are you doing? You're going to go into the railings!'

'No I'm not.' I said. 'I'm going round the roundabout.'

'You're bloody not!' he hissed then he yanked the steering wheel out of my hands to make a sharp right hand turn and we just missed the railings by a millimetre!

I was petrified. One minute I was driving, the next the steering wheel was out of my hands. It was terrifying.

'You bloody stupid bitch!' he yelled as soon as we were safely round the roundabout. 'You're a dangerous driver that's what you are! Now stop here and get out!'

We pulled up and Charlie made me get in the passenger seat while he got into the driver's seat and drove us home.

'You shouldn't be on the roads,' he growled, as I sat there shaking next to him. 'You're a bloody liability!'

I didn't get behind the wheel of a car again for another two years, and thanks to Charlie's disastrous lessons, it would take another five years before I finally had enough confidence to pass my test.

A few months later I woke up feeling sick. I knew what it was but I hoped and prayed I was wrong.

'I'm going to the doctor's,' I said to Charlie that morning. 'I don't feel well.'

'Don't bother,' he replied, obviously thinking the same as me. 'I'll get you a pregnancy test from the chemist's instead.'

He came home at 5 p.m. as usual, threw the chemist's bag on my lap and said, 'Right go on – go and do it.'

So I went upstairs and did the test. When the two small lines came up on the stick, I slumped into a corner of the bathroom and wept.

It was happening all over again. I was isolated alone and depressed – and now I was pregnant again. It just seemed to be a never-ending circle which was only going to get worse and worse and I didn't want it any more.

'It's positive,' I said in a dull voice half an hour later, once I'd managed to calm down and wash the tears off my face.

Charlie grinned from ear to ear then wandered off to the kitchen, not saying a word to me. Another child meant another avenue of control over me, it was the best news he could have had.

He had his plan as usual – we changed doctors again and I was to tell this doctor the same lie I'd told about Alex's father. I'd met a boy at a party and slept with him.

At work Charlie boasted to his colleagues that I was pregnant – and because they all thought we were in a happy relationship they showered me with congratulations when Charlie took me round in his car. I put on a big fake smile and accepted their words silently. How could they know I was dying inside?

Now my life became even more complicated – and the lies were growing every day.

Chapter 9

Tammy

'It's a girl,' the sonographer turned to me with a smile.

For a moment my heart lifted – a girl!

I was secretly hoping it would be a girl. '*If it's a girl, she'll look more like me,*' I thought. '*Then she'll be mine, not Charlie's.*'

I was still struggling to bond with Alex because he was the spitting image of his father so now, at the twenty-weeks scan, I was thrilled to hear I was expecting a little girl.

The sonographer's face suddenly darkened. 'Hang on a minute, I need to get the doctor.'

My joy quickly turned to panic – what was wrong?

The sonographer came back with the doctor and once more passed the scanner over my belly – first picking out my baby's limbs and torso, then the head. I could feel Charlie's beady eyes watching the scanner pass over my body.

The doctor nodded quickly then turned to me and Charlie.

'I'm afraid there's too much fluid on your baby's brain,' she said. 'It's a condition called hydrocephalus.

At this stage we can't be certain how this will affect her but we'd like to do an amniocentesis to check for Down's syndrome.'

'What's an amniocentesis?' I asked, petrified.

'It's a large needle and we use it to take a sample of fluid from around the baby. I'm afraid it carries a small chance of miscarriage, but at least we'll know what we're dealing with.'

'No!' said Charlie forcefully at that point. 'She's not having one of those. If the baby's got any problems then we'll look after her.'

The doctor and sonographer looked at each other – this was coming from the granddad! But I just nodded as if to confirm Charlie's opinion – I certainly couldn't contradict Charlie in front of anybody or there would be hell to pay later on.

So the doctors accepted our decision and I carried on with the pregnancy like there was nothing wrong. Except now I was frightened for my little girl – the doctors had told us the hydrocephalus could make her head grow bigger and squash her brain.

They said when she was born she might need a shunt in her head to drain the fluid.

On top of that, they'd told me that because I'd previously had a C-section, a normal delivery could put pressure on my scar and cause it to burst.

Now, Charlie wasn't just ruining my life, he was threatening the life of an innocent child not even born. I had absolutely no control over my body. He had infiltrated every part of me – his baby was in my belly, his voice was in my mind, the fear he induced was constantly clamped around my heart.

I had the most terrible nightmares which would leave me bathed in sweat and shaking with fear. The same one popped up time and time again – I was shopping in Asda, pushing the trolley round the aisles when my waters broke. The next minute I was having contractions and all of a sudden my previous scar would rip open and all my insides would cascade out of my body onto the floor. I'd desperately try to grab the slippery, bloody innards, but I couldn't reach down far enough and so I was lying there, dying in agony on the floor in Asda when I'd wake up with a start. I'd lie in bed then, weeping with relief and fear.

I needed someone to talk to but I had no one. Certainly Charlie wasn't interested in what I was feeling inside – besides, he was the root of my problems. So I learnt how to deal with all my fear and worries on my own.

But at night, when I couldn't hold it in any more, I'd cry myself to sleep.

I'd learned how to cry silently without waking Charlie up – I'd crawl over to the very edge of the bed then just let the tears flow.

And I did feel better afterwards, if only a little bit.

Sometimes I got migraines afterwards but it was my only release, the only way I had to relieve the fear and the strain.

I was now going for weekly scans and check-ups at the hospital but the doctors couldn't tell if the baby was going to have anything wrong with her so they let me progress with the pregnancy as normal.

Even my blood pressure was all right, compared with how high it had been with Alex.

'Look, we don't know what to expect when she's born,' they kept warning me. 'You can try for a normal delivery but if there are any problems we'll have to step in. Afterwards, we'll send her to a specialist at another hospital to check her over.'

I was hoping everything would be all right because I wanted to give birth naturally this time – I knew that if I had any chance of bonding with my second baby I had to feel like I'd delivered her into this world.

A few weeks before the birth Charlie came home with a TENS machine, an electrical device that helps reduce the pain of contractions, which he'd borrowed off Malik.

Neither of us knew how it worked so we got it out of the pack and put the sticky pads on Charlie's back.

Unknown to both of us the machine was turned up to the highest setting so when he told me to turn it on,

Charlie got a massive electric shock and he leapt off the settee, shouting: 'Oh, shit!'

I sat there, pressing the button over and over again, enjoying every second of his pain. But he just ripped the pads off and threw them on the floor.

I hadn't laughed so much in ages! Although it felt good to laugh, it was strange hearing that sound emerge from my mouth, and the sensation of a smile felt odd on my lips. My laughter was short-lived though, a look from Charlie told me that I was on dangerous ground, so I stopped. However, the thought of hurting Charlie even just a little bit, kept me going for weeks.

Two weeks later I woke at 5 a.m. with these really strange pains, which eventually got worse and worse. This was it: I was going into labour and naturally this time.

We put the TENS machine on me which helped a bit then, when Charlie's mum arrived to look after the children, he drove me to hospital.

There, they gave me gas and air for the pain and all of a sudden I seemed to float away in my own little world where there was just me and the baby. As soon as it wore off though I'd spot Charlie again, skulking round the room, and I'd take another few gasps, just to send me back into that world without him.

But as the hours passed, the pain just got worse and worse and after a while the gas and air didn't seem to make any difference. With Alex I'd only been allowed to have a few contractions before they gave me the C-section so I'd never before experienced the full range of labour pain. And it was hell!

I'd never known anything like it and the screams escaped out of me, without me even realising.

'Oh God, oh God,' I wailed. 'Get this baby out of me. I can't cope any more.'

Charlie didn't want to know. 'Oh shut up will you, it's not that painful,' he snapped. 'Everybody does it.'

I was in so much pain I didn't think before I opened my mouth to reply, 'Well you try sitting here and doing it!'

Then he shot me that look he always gave me whenever he thought I'd crossed the line – the look that could make me shrink with fear and dread.

'Don't even go there,' he growled threateningly.

The midwife was in the room at the same time and as he said that, I glanced at her, wondering if she'd heard. After all, he was meant to be my father. Dads weren't meant to talk to their daughters like that, especially not in labour!

She heard all right. She looked at me then she looked at Charlie and I saw the question passing over her face: '*What the hell is going on here?*'

Eventually they gave me an epidural and I was six hours in labour before Tammy arrived. As soon as she popped out they put her straight on my chest and I looked down at her, for the first time feeling like a proper mother. She was so perfect and so tiny and I thought, '*This isn't Charlie*'. She didn't even look like him, she was beautiful.

She was ten days early so she only weighed five pound fourteen ounces when she was born and this time I managed to breastfeed. But best of all, Tammy didn't look any different from any other baby – she was assessed a few weeks later at the children's hospital but they couldn't find anything wrong.

And for the first nine months of her life, I loved being a mother. We bonded well and even though Charlie was still in control, telling me when I could and couldn't pick her up, I felt close to Tammy in a way I'd never felt with Alex.

I'd creep into her room at night then rest my head on the side of the cot and stare at her for ages, sleeping peacefully.

'I'm going to be a proper mum to you,' I whispered. 'Not like my mum. I'm going to look after you, give you a proper life. Let you know how much I love you, all the time.'

Deep down I wondered if I could ever fulfil these promises to my daughter, give her the love my mum had always denied me, but I tried to shake these niggling doubts from my mind. I watched Charlie like a hawk every time he picked her up or cuddled her – I was terrified that he would hurt her in some way, and

I was screaming inside that this poisonous, rotten human being was touching my pure, innocent little girl. Although, after sometime, I began to realise he actually seemed very protective of our daughter and genuinely cared about her. It seemed I was the only one who could bring out his nasty side and it made me blame myself once again.

For the time being, I had put thoughts of escape out of my mind and for now I was enjoying my little baby. I just prayed that she would grow up knowing her mummy's love.

Of course now I had three children to look after and staying on top of the housework became more and more difficult. Charlie had a habit of turning up at odd times of the day so I had to be careful to make sure that the place was always tidy, however tired I was.

Meanwhile Daniel was pushing the boundaries, just like all kids do as they grow up. Sometimes, when Charlie was out of the house, he'd snatch Alex's toys away or slap him for no reason.

If I tried to tell Charlie, he didn't want to know.

'He's done nothing wrong,' he'd contradict me. 'Leave him alone.'

But I couldn't ignore Daniel's bad behaviour and one afternoon, Alex was playing on the floor when Daniel came up behind him, picked up his toy truck and threw it.

Alex started bawling so I picked him up to comfort him then sent Daniel to bed as punishment.

Ten minutes later Charlie walked in the front door. After his usual sweep of the rooms, he looked about, bewildered.

'Where's Daniel?' he demanded.

'I sent him to bed because he was naughty,' I replied.

'You've got no right to do that,' he snarled at me then shouted upstairs for Daniel to come down.

Obviously thinking he was still in trouble, Daniel slunk into the living room, his eyes cast down in fear at getting a telling off from his dad.

But Charlie wasn't about to tell his favourite little boy off. Instead he walked over to him, tussled his hair affectionately and said, 'You're all right, lad. Come on, here's a tenner. Go get yourself some toffees from the shops.'

I sighed in utter defeat. Charlie was actually rewarding Daniel's bad behaviour and I was made to look like an idiot again.

Daniel was still smiling as he ran out the door but I was seething. For all intents and purposes I was his mum and yet I couldn't discipline him. Here I was, to an outsider looking in, a normal young mother with three children to raise. But scratch the surface and there was a terrified teenager who was bringing up her half-brother like a son, as well as looking after her children who were also, in a way, her stepbrother and -sister. It was a nightmare situation, one that Daniel wasn't even aware of – and I almost felt sorry for the lad – he would grow up thinking this was normal but it was appalling. It's only in hindsight that the full twisted horror of it all has hit me.

I was still confined to the house only now, with three kids in tow, it was driving me up the wall. Every single morning I'd hear the ker-chunk of the deadlock as Charlie slammed the door, just like a jailer, locking up his prisoners. We were like a ghost family – instead of the children being out and about, enjoying their lives, here we were, seeing the world through our locked windows, existing but not really living.

I'd begged Charlie for a key time and time again but he was adamant.

'What do you need keys for?' he'd sneer. 'You've got nowhere to go!'

One day in January, when Charlie was out, I finally snapped. I knew I had to get out of the house or I'd go mad. Daniel had gone round to his friend's house and it was a beautiful, crisp winter's day. Tammy was now eight months old and we had one of those old fashioned Silver Cross prams with giant wheels.

'Come on,' I said to Alex. 'Let's go to the park. You can ride on the wheels underneath.'

I knew I was taking a massive risk – after all, once the door shut behind me I had no means of getting back into the house and once Charlie was home, he'd have a go at me. But I had my excuse all ready. I decided to tell him that I was hanging up the washing outside when the back door slammed shut and we got locked out.

The park was only ten minutes up the road and once there, we had a lovely time. I bounced Tammy on my knee while Alex raced around in the sunshine. We went to the playground and had fun on the swings and I even got chatting to another mum called Fiona – for the first time in years I felt like a normal person, just doing normal things. For once in my life I could pretend that I too was like Fiona, with a handsome husband who loved me and cared for my children. In fact, almost equally appealing, was the thought of being a single mum – no man to tell me what to do! That sort of freedom seemed for ever out of my reach.

It was such a lovely afternoon the time just slipped by and before I knew it was 4.45 p.m. so I bundled Tammy up, put her in the pram and tried to get Alex to come back with us.

'I don't want to go,' he wheedled.

'I know, I know, but we've got to get back,' I said, the panic now gripping my stomach. 'Look, you can ride underneath the pram again. Just please, we have to go.'

In the end I stuck Alex under the pram just to get him to come with me but by the time I got back, Charlie's car was already in the drive and my heart started pounding. The blood rushed to my ears and my brain just seemed to shut down – I couldn't think! And the more I realised that I couldn't think, the worse it got.

What was I going to say? If we'd got locked out I should have been there at the door, waiting for him. How could I explain being away from the house? I couldn't say I was going to the shops because I had no money on me. I was paralysed with fear.

Charlie had left the back door open and was waiting for me in the living room when I walked in, all flustered.

'Where have you been?' he said, his voice low with barely controlled rage. The anger in his voice suddenly unlocked my brain and finally I thought of an excuse.

'Daniel went out but he didn't say where he was going so I had to go look for him,' I said quickly. Now my panic looked like genuine concern for Daniel.

He thought for a minute before replying: 'Okay. Have you done the bedrooms upstairs?'

'Yeah.'

'Have you done the bathrooms?'

This went on in the usual vein but inside I was breathing a huge sigh of relief – I'd got away with it!

For a short while at least.

Two hours later Daniel wandered into the house while I was preparing dinner for the kids. Charlie had told me what to make as usual – chips, sausages and beans. I was never allowed to decide what to give them myself.

I'd just finished feeding Alex and had left Daniel's food on the side when Charlie confronted Daniel.

'Where have you been?' he yelled. 'Why didn't you tell anybody where you'd gone?'

Daniel looked confused and my heart started pounding again.

'What do you mean?' he said. 'I've been to my friend's house. I told Mum where I was going.'

My legs felt weak beneath me but I pretended not to hear this exchange – instead I just carried on washing up the plates, terrified of what was coming.

'All right,' said Charlie. 'Go and eat your dinner.'

I turned to hand Daniel his plate and as I did I glanced over to Charlie and the look on his face was a portrait of fury. He waited just long enough for Daniel to take his food to the table then threw himself at me and whacked me with all his might across my face.

'Why the fucking hell did you lie to me?' he shouted. 'Don't you ever lie to me again, you bitch!'

Alex was in the kitchen, finishing up his plate, and the shock of what he'd just seen made him burst into tears. So Charlie walked over to him and slapped him across the face.

I wanted so much to go and comfort him but I knew if I even moved a muscle towards Alex, Charlie would come flying at us both again. So I just stood there, holding my stinging cheek, frustrated and helpless, while my son bawled his eyes out. His pitiful cries pierced my heart.

Meanwhile, Daniel sat silently at the table.

'This fucking house is a mess,' Charlie said, before he walked out. 'Clean it up!'

So I went round the house cleaning again that evening, my cheek inflamed with pain. The handprint was there for a week.

Everything was fine with Tammy until she reached nine months.

Then, at a routine check-up, the doctor found her liver and spleen were enlarged. Usually, you can't feel the liver and spleen because they are tucked up under the ribcage, but Tammy's were so abnormally big, you could feel them through her distended tummy.

That evening we took her home but she started to run a high fever and had bad diarrhoea all through the night. By the morning she was no better – she wasn't feeding and she was being sick, and her skin had turned a funny brown colour. We were due back at the doctor's later that day but in Tesco's that morning, she suddenly started to have problems breathing so we rushed her straight to the GP.

The doctor took one look at her and phoned for an ambulance to get her to hospital. But Charlie didn't think anyone knew better than him and thought we should take her in the car to the children's hospital in the next town.

'No,' said the female doctor forcefully. 'Don't take her there. It's an hour's drive – she's not going to make it in time.'

But Charlie didn't want to be told different by anyone, especially a woman, and he certainly didn't like being out of control.

'Fine,' he said. 'You wait for the ambulance then and I'll take the kids.'

It was only a matter of minutes before the ambulance screeched to a halt in front of the doctor's surgery but by then Charlie had already left.

Now Tammy was barely breathing and her lips were going blue. The paramedics snatched her off me, ran to the ambulance and put her on oxygen. We arrived at the hospital in less than five minutes and she was rushed straight to the children's medical unit. I sat there, in the waiting room, crying my eyes out, praying she would make it.

Eventually, after an agonising forty-minute wait the doctor came out.

'We tried to get a cannula to get some fluids into her but all her veins had collapsed,' he explained. 'It's because she's severely dehydrated. So we had to do another procedure – we inserted a needle into the bone of her foot which took the liquids straight into her bone marrow and we pumped fluids into her that way. She's stable now.'

I finally breathed out when he said that – meanwhile, Charlie was silently pacing the room. Eventually he muttered under his breath, 'We shouldn't have brought her here. We should have taken her to the children's hospital.'

The doctor turned to him and said, 'And if you'd done that, your granddaughter would be dead right now. By the time you'd got to the motorway, not even the hospital, she'd have been dead.'

Charlie wasn't impressed. 'Yeah, whatever,' he scoffed.

I couldn't believe it – Charlie didn't seem to have a thought for Tammy's life, it was all about him knowing better than everyone else. This doctor had saved our daughter's life and he showed absolutely no gratitude. Fury rose up in me and I had to dig my fingernail into my palms to keep myself from roaring at Charlie in rage. At that moment I saw him the way the doctor must have seen him – like a complete moron.

Tammy was in hospital a week and I stayed with her that whole time, sleeping on a pull-out bed next to her. In some ways it was the best time of my life. I could be with my baby every second without Charlie ordering me about or telling me what to do. Charlie came to the hospital every day to visit, but most of the time he was at home looking after Alex and Daniel.

The nurses came in and helped but it was me who administered Tammy's medicines and changed her – she wouldn't let anyone else do it!

But after a week the doctor came to me. 'We're transferring Tammy to the children's hospital. We think she might have cancer or leukaemia.'

Suddenly the room started to spin and I put my hands up to my face to try and control my tears – I couldn't believe my perfect baby might have cancer. She couldn't die – what would I do without her?

In the ambulance on the way to the children's hospital, the nurse next to me said, 'Look, I need to prepare you for what you're going to see. There are going to be kids in this hospital who are severely ill or dying. That's not an easy sight. Try and prepare yourself.'

I nodded as she spoke but I don't think anything could have prepared me for what I saw when I walked onto that ward. The poor children in there were so ill and frail – many of them had no hair, some were just lying there unconscious with drips in their arms, tubes going into their noses, all hooked up to the machines.

Then I looked at Tammy as they were wheeling her in, so ill and so fragile. Her skin was unhealthily pale, and her body was weak and floppy.

I couldn't take it any more and I ran out sobbing.

The nurse followed me out.

'I'm so sorry,' she said, when she caught up with me. 'I tried to make it easier.'

'I know,' I sniffed, still reeling from the traumatic sight I'd just witnessed. 'But nothing can prepare you for that.'

She nodded: 'Yes, I can understand that.'

*

Tammy was in the hospital for two days while the doctors carried out a series of tests on her – she even had a lumbar puncture to test the fluid in her spine and they gave her a blood transfusion which sent her bright red.

Charlie still visited every day but on the whole I was alone with Tammy, now sleeping on a chair next to her bed, which left my back sore every morning. My fear of Charlie had been replaced by one far more primal and terrifying – the fear of losing my beloved daughter. Finally, the senior doctor approached me – my heart was in my mouth.

'I've worked on this ward for fifteen years,' he started. 'And this is the first piece of good news I've ever been able to give somebody.'

Then he smiled: 'It's not cancer and it's not leukaemia.'

My heart just soared. I burst out crying and I couldn't stop thanking him. He was grinning away like a schoolboy.

That day we were transferred back to our local hospital and she spent another four weeks there, recovering. In the end they told me she'd had glandular fever. It's usually a condition found in much older kids and teenagers, not babies. Nobody could tell me how she got it but she did – and it nearly killed her.

That month, though painful at times, was probably the best of my life. In hospital Tammy and I were free from Charlie – no more cleaning, beatings or sex. I'd felt truly free.

Chapter 10

Hospital

The glandular fever turned out to be just the start of Tammy's problems.

It turned out that Tammy did have fluid on the brain but when we went to the specialist she said it wasn't causing her any problems. But then she started to develop absent seizures – one minute she'd be fine, the next she would collapse on the floor and when she came round she'd be dopey and disorientated.

She was also partially sighted since her eyes didn't produce tears and they'd dry up at night. Later we found out she had speech and language problems and learning difficulties. On top of all that she had terrible bowel problems, which meant we were getting through about thirty nappies a day. Poor little thing, she was such a sweet little girl but so overwhelmed with difficulties. Nothing was straightforward for her – and yet despite all these problems, nobody could tell us what was caus-ing them. She went for every test possible but still we had no firm diagnosis and in the end, when Tammy was three, we were referred to a geneticist.

*

For some reason, the GP's notes were never transferred to the hospital where the geneticist was based so all he knew was that Charlie was my partner, not my stepdad. Even so, it was a very weird day when we had to go to the geneticist.

More and more people were becoming involved in Tammy's care and Charlie just didn't know how to handle it any more, but he couldn't refuse to go to the specialist or he would be seen to be neglecting his daughter's health needs.

To this day, I can't understand why nobody ever put two and two together. After all, the hospital knew Alex was my son, they knew my real age too, so if I was his mother I would have had to have been pregnant at fourteen.

We went along for the appointment with all the kids in tow – Daniel, Alex and Tammy – and Charlie told the geneticist that I was stepmum to Daniel but real mum to the other kids. I was dying for the doctor to ask the identity of Daniel's real mum or my mum for that matter – but he never did, luckily for Charlie, otherwise he would have been found out then and there.

The geneticist concluded that because all the kids resembled Charlie instead of me, it was likely the kids had more of his genes than mine and therefore the problem was likely to be on his side. This made me feel sick. Everyone knew that Alex and Tammy were Charlie's kids – the resemblance was uncanny – so my children were more his, genetically, than mine. It was a horrible thought.

The geneticist took blood samples from Charlie and Tammy. Unfortunately the gene tests came back inconclusive so we were still no wiser as to what was causing her problems. And strangely, I was never tested. Charlie saw this as proof that he wasn't the problem, that Tammy's difficulties came from me. It was yet another stick to beat me with.

Meanwhile, Charlie found a way of getting round the difficult question of our medical records once and for all – when Tammy was four he changed GPs again and because they were a set of GPs he was friendly with through his work, he managed to make them take us on without our previous notes.

So now everyone in the area knew us as a couple and the fact that I was Charlie's stepdaughter disappeared from our lives altogether. Within the space of seven years, Charlie had managed to completely eliminate the past. Now, nobody knew the truth except me and I became even more trapped in the twisted world Charlie had created for us.

The only times I could escape from living under his brutal regime were the occasions I had to take Tammy into hospital. With her problems, she could be in hospital for weeks on end and I always went to stay with her.

Now nobody will tell you that having a sick child is easy but, in terms of my life at home, I have to admit, it was blissful. Away from Charlie, I was free from the tyranny of the non-stop housework, free from his beatings and of course free from the nightly sex demands.

It sounds awful but when we were at home I wished Tammy would get ill again so we could go back into hospital.

Charlie didn't like me being out of the house, of course – sometimes he'd order me to come home and just leave the staff to do the work. But I wouldn't abandon my daughter.

Tammy only let me change her dressings and she hated the nurses coming in with their blue pinnies. It got to the point where she knew a blue pinnie meant pain so she'd scream her head off whenever she saw one. In the end the nurses had to take them off whenever they came near her so she wouldn't get upset.

Coming home again after a few weeks away with Tammy always brought me down.

Charlie was constantly having a go at me for the state of the house and saying that it wasn't clean. During these yelling fits, I'd just zone out and let my mind wander off into space. He'd be screaming while I sat there, staring into space like a zombie, letting it all wash over me.

Outside of the home or hospital visits, I had no life at all, apart from on the rare occasions Charlie insisted

I sit in his car when he ran some errands. I'd be stuck in the car with Tammy while Charlie visited the chemists and dropped off prescriptions or went to the Post Office.

Occasionally he'd let me get out and I'd go into the chemist's with him. There, I'd see a couple of the staff and they were always very nice to me, asking how I was. I'd put on my fake smile and say everything was fine, and I think people honestly thought that was true.

That fake smile was permanently fixed to my face during the day then at nights, I'd burst out crying. That became the way I coped with my life.

By this time Alex was getting older and cheekier to me and it was getting harder to deal with him. The truth was, with all the kids, I felt more like a nanny than a mother. Charlie never let me give them affection or cuddles and he never let me discipline them either – or even decide what to dress them in or what or when to feed them. In truth, I don't think he ever saw me as 'the mum' or even an adult – to him I would always be his daughter and so I didn't have the same rights as him.

So I did my 'mothering' chores in the same way I did all my other chores, with numb compliance.

Then, as the kids got older I seemed to drift away from them – even with Tammy. The worst thing was, even though Charlie was the one who'd smack them and shout at them, the kids loved Charlie far more, it seemed, than they loved me.

Alex would always give him a kiss before bed and if he was upset he'd go to his dad. At the time I didn't understand it – how could they love him when he was so horrible to them and yet they didn't love me?

But then, I wasn't allowed to give them any love so they never expected it from me.

Even as Tammy grew older I felt the bond between us slipping away and there was nothing I could do about it. My barriers started to go up and I felt myself detaching from her. It wasn't until recently I discovered that this stems from the abuse I suffered as a child – and I know I still have to work hard at fighting off those demons from my past. It was only little things at first – like I couldn't bathe the kids as they got older; I couldn't even go into the bathroom when they were there. Now I know, through counselling, this goes back to the time Charlie raped me while I was in the bath, but back then I had no idea the trauma this had left.

So in the end it was left to Charlie to bathe the kids. He gave Tammy her baths at night, changed her if she had an accident and cleaned her bum. It never occurred to me for a minute that he'd abuse her, I guess because I thought she was his real daughter, not like me, his stepdaughter. Also, I thought that what I had suffered was peculiar to me. I must have done something wrong to warrant this kind of punishment.

I'd brought it on myself and was to blame, therefore it was me who would suffer a lifetime of pain. After all those years of Charlie telling me so, I really believed that everything that had happened was my fault, and the only way I could ever escape was in a body bag.

Charlie meanwhile was getting harder and harder to live with. My life was one big lie, but with each passing day, he seemed to embroil me in a new lie.

Charlie was a convincing and well-practised liar in all areas of his life. He worked cash in hand for Malik, all the while claiming disability benefits for his bad back.

When Tammy was four and a half he got a letter from the social saying he had to go for a medical assessment to find out whether he was fit to work. The assessment was twenty miles away so Charlie drove us there and then I 'helped' him walk into the building while he limped along, faking his bad back. I had to pretend I was holding him up as he scowled and grimaced like he'd never known such pain in all his life. It was the performance of a lifetime!

They bought it hook line and sinker. Afterwards, I helped him hobble out, but as soon as we turned the corner he straightened up and strode back to the car where he drove us home again.

He'd managed to fool everyone and I really thought I'd never get anyone to see beyond his lies.

*

Thankfully, for the first time in my life I was allowed to take contraception. This was how little control I had over my body – I couldn't even take medicine without Charlie's approval, and whether or not I was 'allowed' to have children was up to him. In any case, after we'd visited the geneticist he advised us not to have any more children until they got to the bottom of Tammy's problems.

That was a huge relief – I didn't want any more children. I couldn't even cope with the ones I had now. At first I tried the contraceptive patch but that kept peeling off so the doctor gave me the contraceptive injection, which was fantastic.

The only problem was my weight ballooned. At five foot six, I was now back up to twenty stone. Of course I hated it and tried to lose weight but I didn't really know how. Confined to the house all day, I couldn't take any exercise so in desperation, I'd simply stop eating for a few days. That didn't work either because my body would go into 'starvation mode' and store up fat.

Charlie's abuse never helped either. Practically every day now he told me I was fat and lazy and exactly like my mum.

I didn't like the way I looked and because I never went out, I didn't make any effort with my appearance. I'd sit around in tracksuit bottoms and baggy T-shirts, stuffing myself with crisps and chocolate.

It was a vicious circle: the less I went out, the less care I took with myself, the more I ate and the less I *wanted* to go out. Even if I was walking round Asda, I felt people were staring at me, disgusted by what they saw.

But then the doctor told me he was concerned about my weight and took me off the contraceptive injection. Even then I didn't worry too much about getting pregnant because he said it would take a while for my hormones to settle down again. And I thought by this time I was too fat to get pregnant – I couldn't have been more wrong.

A few months after coming off the injection I felt the familiar nausea rise in my throat as I woke up one morning. Later that day, I sat on the toilet, staring at the positive result, crying my eyes out. I was finding life at home more and more unbearable and we still didn't know what was wrong with Tammy.

What if this child was ill too? How would I cope?

Around this time, Charlie's sister Lizzie came to live with us for a few months while Charlie helped her find a place of her own. It was a strange time because Charlie and his sister didn't get on that well but she'd asked for his help and he'd agreed.

Lizzie and Carol, Charlie's mum, had never questioned my relationship with Charlie – they knew he'd gone from being my stepdad to being the father of my children but they never talked to me about it and for all I knew, it seemed normal to them.

While Lizzie was there, Charlie wasn't as harsh to me. In fact, whenever anybody else was around, he didn't shout or have a go at me so her stay gave me a brief respite from Charlie's rages.

I was still made to have sex with him and play with him before he fell asleep every night but that was something I could never escape.

But on the other hand, with another person living in the house, there was no way of hiding my constant crying.

One day Lizzie caught me sobbing at the sink, my hands still holding the scrubbing brush and plate.

'What's wrong?' she asked. 'Why are you crying?'

'I…I don't know,' I sniffed. Of course I knew why I was crying but I could never admit it to anyone. 'I just feel down all the time, I can't stop crying and I don't know why.'

'I think you might have post-natal depression,' she said. 'Why don't you go to the doctors?'

'I don't think Charlie would like that.'

'Don't worry what he thinks. Look, I'll go with you.'

So she took me along to the doctors one day and I told him about the non-stop crying. He agreed I probably had PND and put me on antidepressants that I could take while pregnant.

In the bathroom that night I fingered the packet of small pills and thought about taking one. Yes, I wanted to feel better but I'd seen what these pills had done to my mum. She'd become addicted and turned into a zombie. I didn't want that happening to me. So I put them away in the drawer and left them there. 'Whatever pain I've got I'll deal with it,' I said to myself. So I just carried on going to my scans and antenatal appointments and tried my best to prepare myself for another child. In truth, I was dreading it. I couldn't think of anything worse than having another baby. When they told us it was a boy, I barely registered. It didn't matter to me. Nothing seemed to matter to me any more.

So the biggest surprise of my life was when Tom came along – and I fell in love.

Chapter 11

Family

When I gave birth to Tom it was the most wonderful thing in the world.

I was only in labour for three hours – not long enough for any pain relief except for gas and air – and when he popped out I was struck by how beautiful he was.

There was no other word for it – he was simply gorgeous and I fell in love.

Unlike Alex, he was put straight on my chest, and unlike with Tammy, he was left there.

I just lay back, looking down at his scrunched-up little face and I felt this rush of overwhelming love, like nothing I'd ever experienced before.

Meanwhile, Charlie was getting impatient. 'Can I hold him?' he asked the midwife.

'No, not yet,' she replied brusquely. 'Let her bond with the baby. It's very important.'

Inside I was laughing – no one ever refused Charlie anything and he didn't like it.

'Right, well, when can she come home then?' he huffed.

The midwife looked up from what she was doing. 'Well, she's had no complications, no pethidine or epidural so she can probably go home in six hours.'

Charlie didn't hang around: 'Right, I'm going then. I'll be back in six hours. Make sure you're ready.'

So Charlie left and I was kept in the delivery suite for the next six hours, which was lovely.

It was one of the nicest rooms in the hospital, painted cheerfully in orange and yellow.

At the side of the bed there was a table with a kettle and everything I needed to make a cup of tea. And for all that time I just stayed there with Tom, marvelling at my perfect little boy.

For those six hours, it was just me and him. He was seven pound thirteen ounces and he was so beautiful I couldn't stop taking pictures of him.

Charlie had given me some money to buy some credit for the TV but instead I went to the hospital shop and bought a baby book because I knew I wanted to record every little detail of Tom's life.

It was such a surprise to feel this way but from the moment he was born I felt close to Tom.

By the time Charlie came to pick us up six hours later I'd dressed my little boy in a pair of blue dungarees with a teddy bear on the pocket and a blue jacket with a hood, which Charlie had bought. And I was completely smitten.

*

It was a time of surprises because a few months earlier, my sister came back into my life.

I hadn't expected it at all – in fact I honestly thought I'd never see her again. I'd been in touch with Paul for a while but I felt that Lisa was lost to me.

When Lisa and Paul were put into the foster home, Paul found it difficult to settle. He felt he was treated differently to Lisa and five years after we lost our mum, when he was fourteen, he came looking for me.

I was woken to the sound of the bell in the early hours one morning and was stunned to open the door and find a bedraggled and exhausted-looking Paul standing there. Unbelievably, he'd got up in the middle of the night and walked twenty miles along the motorway.

'I'm not going back,' he told me after I'd sat him down in the kitchen with a cup of tea.

'Let's just wait and see,' I said. 'They'll be worried about you.'

So I called his foster carer at 2 a.m. and told them Paul was with us. And over the next few days I worked on Charlie to try and get him to allow Paul to stay.

He didn't like it – he wasn't keen on me having family around – but in the end he agreed to a trial period so we enrolled him in a local school and hoped for the best. Paul knew I was in a relationship with Charlie but he and the rest of the family thought it was my choice. Nobody had any idea that the abuse had been going on since I was a little girl. Charlie told Paul not to tell Daniel that they were half-brothers because Daniel thought I was his mum. Daniel knew Paul was my brother so he always called him Uncle Paul. It was all so confusing.

Unfortunately, because of Paul's tumultuous upbringing he had a lot of problems. He started skipping school so I ended up walking him to the gates every morning in an effort to make him stay – but once there he'd just do a runner and wouldn't go back.

It was getting difficult to handle him and eventually Charlie became fed up of all the arguments it caused between the kids.

He laid it on the line. 'It's your brother or your kids. If you choose your brother, you'll never see the kids again.'

I didn't have a choice.

I was devastated when I had to tell Paul the following day that we couldn't look after him any more.

'I'll change,' he pleaded. 'I'm sorry. I'll go to school, I promise.'

But I just shook my head, full of guilt and shame. It broke my heart – Paul had come all that way to find me, his big sister, and now I was turning him away but I didn't have the strength to stand up to Charlie. If I chose my brother, he'd take the children and I'd never see them again.

I told Paul's social worker we couldn't cope with him any more and there was nothing we could do. Paul was weeping on the bench in reception as I walked out and I managed to hold all my tears in until I got in the car, then broke down and cried all the way home. It felt like Charlie had taken my family away from me all over again.

Still, behind Charlie's back, I stayed in contact with Paul and tried to be there for him when he needed me, even if I couldn't have him in my house. He was always running away and getting into trouble until social services moved him to a care home in Wales where he finally settled down and achieved a level of happiness.

Then, one day, he called to say: 'Lisa wants to talk to you.'

My heart leapt into my mouth – I hadn't seen or spoken to Lisa since our mum's funeral five years before. What did she want? Did she hate me?

'What does she want?' I asked Paul. 'What if she hates me? I can't speak to her if she hates me.'

As much as I loved and missed my sister, I couldn't bear the thought of being rejected by her – so if she just wanted to speak to me to have a go at me, then I couldn't face talking to her.

Paul called back a few days later. 'Nah, she doesn't hate you, Tina. She just wants to ask you some questions.'

Paul gave me her number and I contrived a plan to speak to her. I'd managed to get a pay-as-you-go mobile from Charlie a few months previously so we could stay in touch while I was in hospital with Tammy and one night he asked me to go to the garage to get some Coke. It took about half an hour to walk to the garage from our house so I slipped the mobile into my pocket and left. My hands were shaking as I dialled the number.

'Hello Lisa – it's me, Tina,' I started, hesitantly.

'Tina! You called!'

'Yeah, look can you call me back cos I don't have any credit?'

She took my number and within a minute she was on the phone again. I didn't know what to say but that didn't matter because Lisa was tripping over her words trying to tell me all about her life.

It was wonderful to hear her voice after so long – she sounded so grown up, not like the little girl I'd known before. And in that half an hour we caught up on everything that had happened to her since she was taken into care and I told her about my kids. Finally, she got round to asking me about Mum.

'I want to know more about her,' she admitted. 'I don't remember much and I've got so many questions.'

It turned out there was a lot Lisa didn't understand because she was too young – like why she and Paul had been taken into care. She didn't know!

So I filled her in on how our mum neglected them and they were left to forage for themselves, about the times they'd turned up for school in dirty clothes they'd been wearing for days and the way they were just left to roam free because Mum was too out of it to care for them. No one had explained to her that Mum couldn't cope because of her illness and medication.

Then she asked me why I hadn't been in touch – she thought I'd picked Charlie over my family but that wasn't the case. I'd been whisked off to another town and I didn't have any choice in the matter. I couldn't tell her the truth though. I was too afraid to tell even my own sister, so instead I fobbed her off with a story about how I couldn't get on with Mum.

The one thing she didn't ask me about was my relationship with Charlie – I was so relieved. I just didn't know how I could possibly explain it to her. But at least she knew that I still loved her and I'd always wanted to see her but wasn't allowed.

It was a difficult and upsetting conversation. I was waiting for that moment she'd tell me she didn't want to see me but it never came. After another half an hour I was nearly back at the house and told her I'd have to go.

'Can we meet up?' she asked.

The last time I'd seen Lisa was at the funeral and she'd been a little girl – just eleven years old – and now she was sixteen.

I didn't know what I was going to do but I immediately agreed. 'I'll sort something out. I promise.'

*

The next few days I thought long and hard about how I was going to travel the twenty miles to see Lisa without Charlie knowing. By this time I'd managed to get my own set of keys but I had no money and the risk was immense. Still, I couldn't let Lisa down so I came up with a plan.

A week later, I asked Charlie for some money.

'What do you need money for?' he asked.

'I need to get some clothes for the kids,' I replied, trying to seem nonchalant.

He gave me twenty pounds – probably just enough to buy one kid a jacket but at least it was sufficient to get me on the train. Perhaps this was an opportunity to leave, but I was pregnant with Tom, couldn't leave Alex and Daniel and was too afraid of being judged and blamed for my abuse. Even when Charlie wasn't physically present, he was always in my mind, and I could not escape from him there.

The next day, after Charlie left for work and Alex and Daniel went to school, I snuck out of the house with Tammy and my twenty-pound note. It was the first time I'd left our town on my own for any reason and I was petrified.

What if we got caught? I dreaded to think how Charlie might react if he knew I was leaving the town altogether but at the same time I felt a rush of excitement. It was like I imagine a prisoner must feel on day release from prison – taking the first tentative steps outside, then the feeling of freedom, of not being answerable to anyone, if only for a short time. But just like that day-release prisoner, hanging over me was the fact that I had to go back to my cell that evening, willingly step through those doors again and have them locked behind me. The fear of Charlie tracking me down and killing me meant I'd definitely be home that night.

We took the bus to the train station then it was an hour's journey and another forty minutes on the bus to where my sister lived. My heart was pounding the whole time but I tried to distract myself by playing with Tammy and looking out the window.

All the while, I was calling Lisa who told me where to get the bus and which stop to get off at. I was nervous as hell as we pulled up to her stop but I saw Lisa immediately.

I hadn't expected to recognise her after all this time but there was no mistaking the familiar large eyes and heart-shaped face – except now she was a grown woman, not a little girl – and her nervous smile of anticipation told me she was as happy to see me as I was to see her.

I got off the bus and we fell into each other's arms, weeping tears of joy. We must have stood there hugging for ages but I didn't care – I never thought I'd be reunited with my sister and it was wonderful.

Lisa took me back to her house and we just sat chatting for hours. She told me all about her life with her foster mum, Kathleen, who was at work, and it seemed she'd had a good, stable upbringing in the last five years.

The only strange thing was she kept calling Kathleen 'Mum', which confused me.

Then she told me she had a boyfriend called Simon, but her mum didn't like him much and wanted her to end the relationship. But Lisa thought she was in love and was now considering moving into his place. It seems she'd reached a crossroads in her life and I could understand why she suddenly wanted answers about her past.

I just sat there marvelling at this strange yet familiar woman in front of me – I couldn't believe how much she'd grown up, and as she filled me in about her past, I felt a deep sense of sadness that I'd missed so many years of her life growing up.

Part of me envied her too – I wish I had been put into care at the same time. I imagined I'd now be a happy teenager with a boyfriend instead of stuck in Charlie's warped world.

But then there wasn't much point wishing for things that had never happened.

After a few hours I realised I had to go home.

'If I'm late Charlie will kill me,' I told her.

'Can I come back with you?' she asked.

It was a bolt out of the blue but how could I refuse her? So we got back on the train that afternoon and all the way home we tried to think up a plausible scenario which Charlie would accept when he found Lisa sitting in his front room. Lisa knew what Charlie was like; she'd seen his controlling ways so she understood the need to be sneaky. He could never know where I'd been.

'You'll have to say you were in town and we bumped into each other,' I told her.

Fortunately when we got in at 4 p.m. Charlie still wasn't home but Daniel was there. Lisa knew Daniel was our brother, but Daniel himself didn't know – he thought I was his mum. So when he called her Auntie Lisa, she didn't put him right. I still don't know why but Lisa accepted the situation with me and Charlie and never asked questions about it. Perhaps, deep down, she sensed there were some uncomfortable truths there and it was better not to know.

When Charlie walked in an hour later, his chin hit the floor. He recognised Lisa instantly and after a few seconds just staring at her, he turned to me.

'What's she doing here?' he demanded.

'She was in town and she called me and asked to come to the house,' I said. Lisa nodded. I held my breath – it was the flimsiest of explanations but he seemed to buy it.

It was strange – Charlie had brought Lisa up from when she was a little girl so she thought of him as her dad and I think she wanted to see him as much as she wanted to see me. But she was also scared of him.

I wasn't sure how Charlie would react. Having Lisa back in my life gave me some family again and I knew he hated me speaking to anyone.

But he surprised us both – he was very kind and polite to Lisa and agreed to let her stay for a bit.

What Charlie and I didn't know at that point was that Lisa was pregnant too. After a few days at our place she came out with it – she feared her foster mum would be angry.

She was sure Simon would stand by her – but sadly, after just a few months she and Simon went their separate ways and it broke her heart.

Nevertheless, Lisa decided she wanted to stay so she lived in our house for a few weeks before we helped her find a place of her own. We were pregnant at the same time and it was nice having her back in my life. While Charlie was at work we'd go round to each other's houses – I didn't tell him this, of course. Instead, I'd say I had a hospital appointment for Tammy and it was going to last all day – but when it was finished in just a couple of hours I'd visit my sister and spend the afternoon with her, just chatting and drinking tea.

Eight weeks after I gave birth, Lisa went into labour and I was there by her side when Matt was born. It was amazing. I'd only ever been the one *having* the baby before, I'd never seen someone else give birth and it was amazing.

Lisa didn't love it quite so much.

After just two contractions she was begging for every kind of pain relief imaginable!

I couldn't help myself, I burst out laughing.

'Oh honey,' I said. 'This is only just the start. Just pace yourself!'

But I knew exactly what she was going through so I tried my best to be a good birthing partner and when Matt arrived I was so proud of her. No wonder she'd screamed so much – he was a whopping nine pounds seven ounces!

I looked at him and started crying, then I gave her a hug and said, 'Well done!'

She deserved it – he was massive! He didn't fit any of the newborn clothes we'd brought to the hospital and from the moment he was born, he was wearing baby clothes for a three- to six-month old.

He barely fitted into his baby cot – his head was at the very top and his feet were touching the bottom. All the other mums on the ward would stare at her as they cradled their tiny little bundles and she hefted this whopping big baby!

For the next few weeks Lisa and I were always in each other's houses, playing with our babies and enjoying sharing time together. It was like we'd never been apart.

I made up hundreds of different excuses to Charlie, telling him the doctor was late at the surgery or the appointment had been put back. The older I got the wiser I was to getting around Charlie. But, one day Lisa overheard me on the phone lying through my teeth to him and asked afterwards: 'He doesn't like me, does he?'

What could I say? It was true; Charlie, had no grounds, but he worried that Lisa was a bad influence on me and would encourage me to flirt with boys.

'Erm, I don't know,' I mumbled.

'It's okay,' she smiled at me. 'I don't mind. As long as I can see you, it's fine.'

I smiled back at her and we looked down at our little babies lying side by side on a blue quilt on the floor and couldn't help giggling.

Tom was two months older than Matt but side by side, Matt was twice the size.

Chapter 12
Tom

Having my sister around and Tom to look after lifted my depression for a while and for nine, blissful months I found I didn't cry as much and could cope with Charlie's temper tantrums.

But then, just like Tammy, at exactly nine months Tom's skin turned an odd colour.

I knew what it was as soon as I saw it; it was the same as what Tammy had but much, much worse.

We took him to the doctors and they found that he also had a very large liver and spleen and my heart just sank – I knew we were in for the same problems that we'd had with Tammy.

Still the doctors had no idea what was wrong with her – it was like a giant jigsaw puzzle. We had all these little problems but the one piece that was missing was the diagnosis. They'd try and match her symptoms up to established conditions but nothing fitted her completely. Even to this day we still don't have an answer.

Meanwhile, Tom became more and more unwell and eventually I had to take him into hospital. We were there for eight weeks and it was awful because he was in so much pain with his face.

Still, he never complained. He was such a sweet child, we'd just sit on the bed together watching his favourite programme, *The Tweenies*, cuddling and trying to make the best of things.

We were in the hospital three weeks before Tammy had to be admitted too. We were all in one big room together – Tom in the cot, me in a bed in the middle and Tammy in a bed on the other side of me. It was just the three of us, and it felt cosy going to sleep in the same room together like this, as if we were in a cabin on a great big ship. And thankfully, Charlie barely came to the hospital during this time. When he did come, he didn't have any patience with the doctors and nurses, he'd kick off and storm out, so if only for that reason alone it was better that he didn't come.

It was hard having two sick children in hospital at the same time but I have to confess I was more scared for Tom that I was for Tammy. The doctors told me that when she'd caught the glandular fever at nine months, it had given her a little bit of immunity to fight back infection. Tom seemed to have no immunity at all.

Tammy was only on the ward for a month before she could go home but Tom was in there two months. And even then, he was on a huge amount of medication. Annoyingly the doctor at our surgery kept taking him off them so once a month, without fail, I'd have to call up the hospital insisting they gave him his medication and the consultant would then have to call our GP to ask them to prescribe him what he needed.

When Tom was twenty months old we got a letter through the post from our GP saying Tom had to be taken for his MMR vaccine. Now we'd only just come out of hospital from another bout of illness at that point and Tom was full of cold so I called up the surgery.

'Look,' I said. 'I don't think it's a good idea we give him the MMR now. He's got a cold and he's not too well. When he gets a little better we'll bring him along.'

But the surgery wouldn't budge. A week later they sent another letter, insisting I take Tom for his vaccines. And almost every day after that I got phone calls from the surgery, saying I had to bring him along or they would take me to court. I tried to tell them Tom wasn't a well little boy but they were insistent and the legal threats kept coming – by phone, by post and in person.

Eventually, I didn't know what to do so I asked Charlie.

'Oh, just take him, will you?' he said. 'He's got to have it eventually so just get on with it.'

So a few days later I was at the surgery with the health visitor.

'They usually develop a little rash after a week,' she explained. 'But that's normal, nothing to worry about.'

176

So I sat there, holding Tom on my knee while she stuck the needle into him and he screamed blue murder.

Seven days later we were back at the hospital. Tom's whole body was covered in tiny red dots, completely covering him so he looked like a beetroot. I was terrified. They did a series of tests on him and when I asked what was wrong they told me straight.

'We know what's wrong with him,' said the doctor. 'He's got measles, mumps and rubella.'

Tom had no immunity so he couldn't fight off the vaccines. His white blood cells were down to zero and his iron levels were so low, they had to give him an iron drip.

For two weeks I watched as my little boy deteriorated – he wasn't eating or drinking and just seemed to be getting weaker and weaker.

Finally the doctor came to me. 'Nothing's working,' he said. 'I suspect the only way we have to wipe out the illnesses would be to give him a bone marrow transplant. He'd have to have chemotherapy first – and that will wipe out his immune system but also get rid of the measles, mumps and rubella. We'll have to transfer him to the children's hospital for that.'

'Oh God, no,' I moaned.

I couldn't bear the thought of going back to that place – it held such bad memories for me of when Tammy was ill. But we didn't have any choice.

Luckily they were redecorating the children's ward at that time so when we first arrived Tom was put in an isolated cubicle. There, they did loads of tests and a lumbar puncture revealed he had a condition that affected the immune system and Tammy probably had the same thing. But while the glandular fever had given her some small immunity against the MMR vaccine, Tom had none at all.

After two weeks at the hospital, the immunologist came to me. 'We're going to start him on chemo. It will wipe out his immune system but then we can build it back up again. I'm afraid there's only a forty per cent chance of survival.'

I couldn't bear it any longer. Worse, by now I was thirty-three weeks pregnant with my fourth child. It sounds weird, but carrying my stepfather's children had become second nature to me and with everything that was going on with Tammy and Tom, I must admit at times I almost forgot I was going to be a mother again.

During my other pregnancies I'd fretted about Charlie's child growing inside me, that it meant the sinister secret he made me keep would come out and my life would be in danger. Already numb to the daily abuse I was forced to endure – even while pregnant – it all faded from my consciousness this time. And for one reason: my beautiful baby boy was ill. Seriously ill.

*

As the days passed, I watched helplessly as my son got weaker and weaker – by now he could barely stand and couldn't walk. He used to lie in his cot and cry but no sound would come out.

He was literally dying in front of my eyes and there was nothing I could do about it. I was distraught – poor Tom had had a tragic start in life due to circumstances out of his control and now he had to go through painful and exhausting chemotherapy. He was just getting worse and worse. Charlie left me on my own most of the time as he had to look after the other children.

Desperate to try and build Tom up, I'd sit in the little cafeteria with him every day, trying to encourage him to swallow a few mouthfuls of Weetabix mashed with full fat milk and tonnes of sugar. But he could barely keep his head up.

For weeks I sat by his bedside, willing him to get stronger, praying that he'd manage to fight off the diseases. And over time, I saw a small improvement.

He gradually regained the ability to stand up, walk while holding my hand and kick a ball about. Then the refurbishment was completed and we were moved back to the ward.

Now, we were on the ward with other children with cancer and leukaemia and all their visitors kept coming in, bringing with them colds, viruses and infections. It was a disaster – Tom had no immune system so he caught everything.

He ended up with thirty-two different infections and this made him really ill. We spent six weeks in total on that ward – I'd still sit with him on the bed watching *Tweenies* for hours but I could tell he wasn't improving.

They were giving him daily blood and platelet transfusions but then he stopped eating and drinking completely. I had to beg for them to put a feeding tube down him.

It was me who held him down while he screamed and the doctor put the tube down his nose.

'It's going to help you,' I soothed, my voice cracking with emotion. 'Please, love, just stay still. It'll make you better.'

But it never did. After that he developed a bad nose bleed and lost a lot of blood. By now he was twenty-two months and they were pumping blood into him every day.

I'd been up with him for two days and nights straight and was absolutely exhausted. I remember him sitting there in the cot, crying and moaning.

'Why won't you go to sleep?' I begged. 'Please, just go to sleep.'

But the crying went on and on and after another half an hour I snapped.

'Just go to sleep!' I yelled.

Another twenty minutes passed and suddenly there was silence. '*Thank God,*' I thought. He's finally gone off.

But then I heard a strange gurgling noise coming from the cot – Tom's breathing had become strained and he was now fighting for air.

I called for the nurse and the team swung into action.

They rushed him into ICU. I remember just sitting there, crying, and scared. I knew he wasn't going to get any better.

'We're going to have to sedate him,' they told me and I nodded numbly.

I was holding his hand as they injected him and at first he had my finger in a really tight grip but then slowly his fingers released, then he let go and he was out of it.

He was put on oxygen, which they kept him on for twenty-four hours, trying now and then to turn the levels down but every time they did that, the level of oxygen in his blood would drop. So he was put on a stronger ventilator and the second day he was there they did another lumbar puncture.

The results revealed the chemo wasn't working. And further blood tests showed his organs were now slowly shutting down.

By now Charlie had joined me in intensive care and the doctor took us to one side and told us the stark truth.

'You have two options,' he said grimly. 'We can either keep him on the ventilator and gradually his organs will shut down and he'll die. Or we can turn off the machine and he'll go quicker.'

I wanted to keep him on that ventilator, I really did. I just wanted to keep him alive as long as I could, but I didn't have any choice.

Charlie answered: 'We'll turn off the machine.'

As he said those words, my body went into shock. I felt a huge sob well up inside me and ran out of the room to the toilets. I called my sister but she could barely understand me I was crying so hard.

'What is it, Tina?' she said. 'Just slow down. Tell me, what's wrong?'

Eventually I managed to get the words out: 'He's dying.' Then I broke down again and Lisa stayed on the phone as I cried my heart out.

After fifteen minutes I managed to calm down enough to wash my face in the toilet sink.

Then I looked up and caught sight of my tired, baggy eyes, my ravaged face and unwashed, greasy hair pulled back into a messy ponytail.

'Pull yourself together,' I told my reflection sternly. 'Your son needs you.'

So I took myself back to the ward where Charlie said he was going to pick up the other kids to come and say their goodbyes.

Meanwhile, I managed to get the hospital priest to christen Tom. Afterwards, I just sat by his bedside, kissing him and telling him I was sorry over and over again. Looking down at his pale little body, my heart ached with pity. I thought I'd felt heartbroken so many times in the past, but this was a pain like no other. Tom had been the only light in my otherwise dark life.

'I didn't mean to shout at you,' I wept, stroking his chubby little hand. The rest of his body was covered with wire and tubes and pads. I knew he was unconscious but I prayed that somewhere he could hear my voice. 'Mummy loves you so much. So much.'

And all the while that my little son Tom was dying, my new baby was kicking and turning over in my tummy. It was such a horrendous situation, it didn't feel real.

Two hours later, Charlie returned with the other kids – they looked scared and uncomfortable. They really didn't know what was going on and seemed confused when we told them to say goodbye to their baby brother. Then they were ushered out by Charlie's sister Lizzie and taken to wait in another room.

It was 8 p.m. by this point and the nurses brought a settee into the cubicle where me and Charlie were waiting with Tom, still hooked up to all the machines and drugs.

The atmosphere was heavy and still.

'Right, we're ready to switch it off,' said the doctor quietly.

I nodded, unable to say a word, and gradually, the nurses started unhooking all the wires and taking out all the drips from his arms. Then they switched off the ventilator, picked him up and placed him in my arms. I kept willing him to take one last breath, just one, and then wake up. But he never did. Slowly, he slipped away in my arms.

When he was gone, I found I was weeping uncontrollably. Looking at his face, he seemed so peaceful, so quiet. It's like all the illness left him at that moment.

And Charlie cried – it was the first time I'd seen him cry.

After that the nurses came in to clean him up. They asked me if I wanted to bathe him but I couldn't do it. I was a mess. All I could think about was shouting at him and telling him to go to sleep. And then two days later he was finally asleep.

Was it my fault he died? Did he go because I told him to? I couldn't help thinking about my mum, and how I had shouted at her before she died. The guilt was immense, overwhelming.

The nurses bathed and dressed him, then they took a hand cast and a lock of his hair for us.

We looked at him again in his cot and he just seemed so peaceful and still, like he was sleeping. He didn't look dead at all but then I picked him up and he was so heavy – I'd never felt anything so heavy in my life.

I couldn't bear to leave him but after a while Charlie tugged at my arm, 'Come on,' he said. 'We have to go home now.'

His voice seemed to come from a distant place, like the sound of a voice on the end of a long-distance call. I knew he was right next to me but I could hardly hear him.

I wasn't really there any more. I was somewhere else. Somewhere far away where nobody could touch me, not even Charlie.

Chapter 13
Thomas

I had felt pain before: I had been continually abused as a child and an adult, I was trapped with a man who controlled me and who made me perform sexual acts with him that I just didn't want to do. I was no stranger to grief. But the pain I felt after Tom had died was harder than anything I had ever experienced.

When Tom died, part of me died with him. I'd loved him to bits and yet he was ripped away from me. The constant heaviness in my heart was unbearable; all the years I'd spent building a wall around my emotions to stop getting hurt came crumbling down.

I couldn't even bear to think about my unborn baby. I didn't want another baby, I just wanted Tom back. I'd have given anything to have him back and hold him again.

The morning after Tom died Charlie said we had to go back to the hospital to register the death. I didn't want to go back there but I did want to see my baby again so I steeled myself to walk back into the hospital.

They had put him in the chapel of rest and we went along with some new clothes and shoes for him – it was all I could think to bring.

When we got to the hospital the doctor gave us his certificate of death and asked if they could do a post-mortem on him.

'No!' I shouted savagely. 'You are *not* going to cut him open. I don't want anyone touching him.'

By now I didn't care what anyone thought – this was my son and they weren't going to do one more thing to his poor, ravaged body.

'Well, there's a good reason for doing it,' the doctor said gently. 'We'd have a better reason for why he died.'

'You know why he died,' I shot back. 'You're not doing it and that's final.'

Afterwards we went into the chapel of rest and there he was, my little boy, lying so peaceful and quiet on the table with a red quilt over him. I lifted up the quilt but the only thing he had on underneath was a babygrow. I felt his body, so cold – I just wanted to make him warm again. So I carefully put on all the clothes we had brought with us.

Then, after I'd dressed him, I placed my finger inside his little palm and got the shock of my life when his hand closed up.

'Oh my God!' I shrieked, then started trembling all over. 'What's happening?'

Luckily, the attendant was there and he reassured me. 'It's just a reaction – it's perfectly normal.'

'He's not alive?' I answered in a tiny, hopeful voice.

'No, I'm sorry, madam,' he said gravely. 'He's not alive.'

Even so, I stood there and held him for ages, whispering to him, telling him over and over again – 'I'm sorry, I'm sorry, I'm sorry'. I didn't want to put him down.

Eventually, Charlie said we had to go and even though I begged for ten more minutes he wouldn't let me stay. So I placed Tom under the red quilt again and reluctantly left him there.

Later that day we visited a funeral director and explained what had happened. We talked about the funeral and what we wanted for the music, the service and the flowers. I picked out a big blue teddy bear for him and Charlie's sister chose an arrangement shaped as the gates of heaven.

Then they went to pick him up and asked me if I wanted to go to the funeral home to visit him there.

'No, you're not going,' Charlie told me.

'I've got to,' I sobbed. 'I've got to see him again.'

'No,' he said. 'It's over. Let him be. It's not fair on you, it's not fair on the baby.'

Once again, even when I was mourning my dead son, Charlie had exerted his power over me.

I wasn't even thinking about the baby I was

expecting at that point. All I could think about was Tom – I didn't want him to be left alone. I wanted him to know I was there for him.

Every second of every day my thoughts were on him and at nights I was consumed with guilt. I'd taken him to get the MMR vaccine when he had no immune system – I felt it was my fault he'd died. If I'd never taken him that day he'd still be with me.

By now the final blood test results were back and they showed that Tom had measles in his system when he died. How could he have got it except through the vaccine? The hospital sent me a letter. It said that Tom had had a severe reaction to the MMR vaccine.

So that was it. I blamed the doctors for pressurising me into taking him along for the vaccination. I understood that they thought it was the right thing and every child should be protected, but I couldn't help but feel angry. Most of all though I blamed myself. I was his mother. I should have stood up to them.

A week after Tom's death we held the funeral but by this point I was so deep in grief, I barely remember being there. Charlie didn't want the other kids to come so he arranged to leave them with a childminder and drove us to the church alone.

Together, we carried the small white coffin up the aisle to the front of the church.

Looking about, I couldn't believe how many people were there – many I recognised as teachers from the kids' schools and the nursing staff from the hospital who'd looked after Tom in his last months. No one knew the truth – that I was Charlie's stepdaughter, not his partner. It was bizarre – we must have looked like a normal family to the people sitting in the pews. But how would they have felt, looking at us both, if they knew that Charlie was at the root of my grief? Would they have seen the schoolgirl, neglected and abused by her mother and then raped by Charlie? Or would they have seen me, the twenty-two-year-old adult, and blamed me for the predicament me and my kids were in? Whatever they would have felt, I know that not one of them could judge me as harshly as I was judging myself.

The woman priest who took the service did a really good job, but I can't for the life of me remember now a word she said.

I just sat staring at that small white coffin in front of me with Tom's picture on top, unable to believe that my sweet little boy was inside it.

At the end they played P Diddy's 'Every Breath You Take' and I wept uncontrollably. Even now I can't listen to that song.

After the service we drove up to the cemetery where we buried my son and threw red roses into the ground on top of the coffin. I didn't want to leave. Tom was gone and there was nothing I could do about it.

Charlie finally steered me away from the graveside and drove us to the pub where we had some drinks. I don't even remember how that day ended. Or the next day…or the next. I was in a terrible state. I just lay in bed crying, day after day. At night, I took sleeping pills to give me a tiny bit of rest. I couldn't turn the pain off or stop my head from thinking dark thoughts. I didn't want to live. All I wanted was to be with Tom.

'Look at the state of this place,' Charlie said to me one morning after I'd managed to drag myself into the kitchen to make a cup of tea. 'Clean this bloody house up, for God's sake, and stop moping about!'

But I didn't. I just went straight back to bed. I didn't care any more what Charlie thought or did. There was nothing he could do that could hurt me any more than I was already hurting. I'd spent my whole life living in fear of him, but now something had changed. I'd experienced the worst fear I ever could – the death of my son.

Losing Tom had taken me to a place in my life I had never even thought existed. You just don't imagine your children will ever die before you. When I lost my mum, I was upset, but it wasn't anything like this.

Charlie started blaming me too for Tom's death, but I never react.

'*Yes*,' I'd think numbly. '*It was my fault.*'

Exactly a week after the funeral I was back in hospital for a check-up. As the midwives noted my blood pressure was high it was decided I should be induced.

They knew all about Tom and the fact that we'd buried him just a week earlier so they put me in a side room on my own. I was sitting there, staring at the grey wintry sky outside, still locked in my private grief when the midwife came in and pulled a chair up next to the bed.

'Have you thought of any names?' she asked me.

'Yeah, I'm going to call him Tom.'

We'd known it was a boy from the first scan but I didn't have any doubt in my mind what his name was going to be.

She looked surprised and sat there for a while, thinking.

Then she said gently, 'That won't be very fair on him, love. He has to have his own individuality.'

'I don't care,' I replied. 'I want him back. I want Tom back.'

'Can I make a suggestion?' she said slowly. 'Why don't you call him Thomas instead? Then he'll be his own person but he'll also have a part of Tom in him.'

I thought about it and decided she was right. That was what I'd call him – Thomas.

So just a week after we'd buried Tom, my third son Thomas was born. Tom had died at 8 p.m. on a Tuesday, we'd buried him on a Tuesday and the following Tuesday at 8 a.m., after a three-hour labour, his brother was born.

And when I held him, he looked just like his big brother Tom.

It's hard to explain now because no one can fully appreciate the depths of a mother's grief unless you've been there yourself but for the first two years of Thomas's life I honestly thought he was Tom.

I looked at him and he was the spitting image. I held him and inside my heart was singing. '*I've got him back*,' I thought. '*I've got my boy back. He's come back to me and he's all better.*'

I wasn't thinking straight, of course I wasn't, but I clung on to that belief for two long years because I could never accept losing Tom.

When I got out of hospital it was a few weeks till Christmas but the house felt alien to me now. Everywhere I looked I saw reminders of Tom – the pram, his bedroom, his toys were all over the house.

We tidied them all away and put them in a cupboard but even that wasn't enough. So eventually I told Charlie we had to get rid of them. I couldn't bear having them in the house any longer.

I went back to the hospital and spoke to the nurse who'd looked after Tom when he first fell ill. I couldn't bear to return to the children's hospital where he'd died.

It was hard walking down those corridors again, there were so many memories of Tom in that hospital, but at least he'd been alive when he was here.

'I've got all of Tom's stuff,' I said. 'Is there any chance I could donate it to the hospital?'

'Of course,' she replied. And then I gave her all of his

toys. It was a relief to finally get them out of the house but there were certain things I couldn't get rid of.

I kept his little brown jumper and a few other little bits and pieces like his pillow, the lock of his hair, the hand cast and even the top I gave birth to him in.

Then I made up a little blue folder in which I placed all his pictures and scans.

Sometimes I'd put his old brown jumper on Thomas and that made me so happy.

He was just like his brother.

When Thomas was six weeks old we took him along to the doctors for his check-up and there they discovered he had a heart murmur.

'We're going to have to transfer him to the hospital for tests,' the doctor said and I just collapsed on the floor. I couldn't stand it any longer. From that moment I was convinced I was going to lose Thomas too. What was going on? Why were all my children falling ill? Charlie blamed me, and I blamed myself – I must have been cursed to have all these horrible things happen to me, one after the other. Had I done something to deserve this? The same thing that meant I deserved to be abused by Charlie too? It was unreal.

Eventually the results came back and revealed Thomas had a condition called aortic stenosis – the main valve to his heart was too narrow and eventually he would need surgery to open the valve or replace it. It was never going to cure itself.

*

Can you imagine telling a mum who has just lost her child that her new baby is ill? I became utterly paranoid and from that moment onwards my whole life became focused on keeping Thomas alive.

The minute I heard a sneeze or cough, I'd rush him to the doctors, nearly hysterical with fear.

They got so sick of me in the end the hospital gave me open access, which meant I could take him straight there if I thought anything was wrong.

Meanwhile, I'd decided to breastfeed him as long as I could – I felt that if he was getting antibodies from me then that would help him fight off infection and boost his own immune system. I ended up breastfeeding him for two years!

My maternal instinct overtook whatever fear I had of Charlie and when it came to Thomas, I had no qualms about standing up to him now.

'Won't you put that bloody baby down?' he'd shout if I picked him up to feed.

'I'll do what I want,' I'd retort. 'I've lost one child, I'm not going to lose another!'

I didn't care any more about the consequences – yes, he could hit me, or shout at me, or worse – and he did – but he couldn't change what I was feeling or what I was going through.

So I picked Thomas up when I wanted and gave him all the cuddles and love that I could – we formed a bond stronger than any I'd had with my other children.

I was still scared of Charlie – he was still demanding

sex, he was still controlling, still shouting and scream-ing and hitting me. But I didn't care so much any more. Whatever pain he gave me – if he hit me, slapped or punched me – it was nothing.

He blamed me for Tom dying. What could be worse? Nothing. He could kill me! That was the only worse pain I could feel. But then, I'd be dead and my problems would be over.

And, increasingly so, that became what I wanted. I wanted to die, I wanted to be with Tom. I used to daydream about killing myself. But just as I was disap-pearing into my fantasy world, I'd hear the cry of a baby or Tammy would come and tug at my top and I'd be filled with a sense of shame.

If I died, who would have them? Who would look after them if I wasn't around? Charlie?

My weekly trips to the hospital had alerted the doctors to the fact that I was still grieving and they wanted to put me on antidepressants but I refused to take them.

'*This is your punishment*,' I'd tell myself. '*This is your pain. You can't just take a pill and block it all out.*'

You see, I wanted to hurt because I believed it was my fault. It was the same thing I'd told myself as a little girl whenever Charlie abused me: I deserved to feel that way.

Chapter 14

Friend

Charlie refused to talk to me about Tom's death – in fact he banned me from mentioning his name in the house. But he couldn't stop the kids from asking questions and one day, when Thomas was three months old, Alex came sidling up to me while I was preparing tea.

'Where's Tom?' he asked me in his childish innocence. 'Why did he die?'

It was the first time I'd heard his name in weeks and just the mention of him was like a stab in the heart. I just burst out crying.

'Where is he, Mum?' he asked again.

'He's gone to heaven, love,' I replied. 'He's not poorly any more and he's better where he is.'

Alex looked at me uncertainly, like he didn't quite believe what I was saying. And ten minutes later Charlie banged in the door to find me sobbing on the sofa.

'Why are you crying?' he demanded to know.

'Alex asked me about Tom, that's all,' I sniffed. 'He asked me where he'd gone.'

'Don't you bloody talk about him,' he said to me.

'And you!' he turned to Alex: 'Don't you be so bloody nosey.'

I couldn't accept that Tom was gone – and I needed desperately to talk about him to someone. I was frightened that if I didn't keep his memory alive, he'd soon be forgotten.

Charlie had recently bought a computer and I went online one day and found a memorial site where you could build a page in memory of the one you've lost.

I told Charlie I was doing it and he didn't mind, at first. Quickly, my every thought was consumed by Tom and I became obsessed with creating this memory page on the Internet. It made me feel Tom was going to live on somehow. And I loved choosing pictures of him and arranging them on the page.

Gradually I got talking to some of the other people online who were building pages for lost loved ones. They'd formed a support group on MSN for bereaved parents and through it I met a nice lady called Diane who'd lost a little girl. We reached out to each other to share our pain.

But our son's death didn't seem to affect Charlie – except to make him more aggressive and controlling. He was always shouting and putting me down and I was getting more depressed by the day. My only outlet for my grief was the computer and the people I'd met there. From the moment I woke up to the time I fell asleep, my every waking thought was of him, and I desperately needed people to talk to about him. And what helped me most was that, through the anonymity of the Internet, I was free to be myself. It was a liberating experience for me.

Charlie had tolerated me building a web page for Tom, but when he realised I was communicating with other people, he quickly put a stop to it.

One morning he got up and unplugged the wires on the computer so I couldn't go on it while he was at work. He hid the wires in the garage but it didn't take me long to find them and plug the computer back in to chat to Diane. When he realised I was still getting online, he started taking the wires to work with him.

I tried to persuade him to let me carry on but he didn't trust what I did on the computer.

'They're just other mums like me who've lost kids,' I'd cry. 'What's wrong with that?'

'Well, let's just see then, shall we?' and then one night he sat there next to me while I chatted to the other women in the group.

As long as it was all women he was fine, and I had to be very careful what I was writing, but then a bloke joined the group and Charlie stopped letting me go on the computer even in the evenings, just another way of cutting me off from the outside world. Another bar in the window of my prison cell.

And that was when I started rebelling against

Charlie. No matter what he did, and in defiance of him, I usually managed to get the computer working again when he was out. It meant a lot to be able to talk to Diane about Tom. It felt like I wasn't alone. And that's why I started making the first tentative steps towards becoming braver. I was gradually realising that I wasn't as scared of him any more – he could hurt me but the physical pain was nothing compared to losing a child. I had just been through the worst thing that I could imagine and Charlie's kicks and punches, his insults, the way he forced himself on me every night, that was something I could live with. I was beginning, in a very small way, to find my strength.

Finally, Charlie came home from work one day to find me on the computer again and he went berserk. He marched over to the computer, unplugged it, locked the router in the car and took it to work with him the next day.

After that, I only got to occasionally go online at the weekends because then Daniel would want to be on it and Charlie let Daniel use it whenever he wanted.

One Saturday I was surfing the net when I stumbled into a spiritualist group. I wasn't into anything religious or spiritual, but I guess I was looking for answers.

They were all just chatting in this forum and I hadn't said a word – I was just sat there reading what everyone else was saying – when the psychic Tricia said she had a little boy coming through to her.

Then she described Tom to a tee – and I just sat at the computer, my mouth open in shock.

'*I think that's for me,*' I typed, my fingers shaking over the keyboard. It was the first thing I'd typed since I'd entered the chat room.

Tricia couldn't have known anything about me – I'd not said a word and there was nobody in that room who knew me either. All she had was my username, not even my real name.

So what she told me next left me absolutely stunned.

She went into details that nobody else knew. She described how Tom died, said he was on a ventilator and she even gave a description of what he was wearing when we buried him. Only three people in the world knew that information – me, Charlie and Charlie's sister Lizzie. But she described it perfectly – it was a tracksuit with white trainers and a babygrow underneath with reindeers on it.

When I saw what she'd written, I choked on huge sobs.

Then she said, '*He doesn't want you to cry.*'

I nearly fell off my chair!

'*How do you know I'm crying?*' I typed.

'*Because your little boy told me. He's happy. He wants you to know that. He's happy that he's not in any pain any more. You've got another little boy named after him.*'

I was stunned – goose bumps rose on my flesh and sweat prickled my scalp. How did she know all of this?

'*Your little one says he's really happy that he's part of his brother and he comes to chat to him at night-times.*'

All of this was freaking me out but it was also so comforting to hear – I just wanted to know he was safe and happy and Tricia's words were like a soothing balm to my troubled soul.

Then she said, '*You sleep with something every single night that belongs to him, something you had when he was in hospital.*'

And it's true – when Tom was in hospital I bought a big blue square Winnie the Pooh pillow. I've still got it to this day and I still sleep with it every night. She described it perfectly.

I've never been religious but I genuinely felt a strong connection with Tricia and she seemed to be able to talk directly to my heart. Tricia lived in Norfolk, and so we never met face to face, but still I could feel her warmth and kindness just as if she was sitting in the same room as me.

It was like I'd been in darkness for so long and for the first time ever, someone was shining a beautiful light onto me. Without ever meeting or talking in person, it was like Tricia had been sent to give me hope and kindness at the very moment I needed it most.

After that day we chatted more online and I gradually opened up to her about my life. I still couldn't tell her about Charlie being my stepdad because despite everything the notion that if I told anyone, he'd kill me had been so deeply drummed into me my brain needed to be rewired to think any other way. I'd lived with the lies for so long now, I didn't even know how to tell her the truth. Even my kids didn't know my real relationship with their father, just that I was their mum and he was their dad, and I guess that was true. They never imagined that I was also their stepsister.

But I did tell Tricia that Charlie was abusive and whenever I felt down or upset she'd just pop up on the computer and tell me to stop crying. Then I'd pour my heart out to her about what awful thing Charlie had said or done to me that day.

Tricia became my closest friend and in time, I would come to look on her as a mother. I honestly believe that if it wasn't for her, I probably wouldn't be here today.

Chapter 15
Going, going...

Now that I had found my friend Tricia, I was on the phone to her regularly. Usually I would call her in tears after another outburst from Charlie or if I was worried about Thomas' health problems. Hearing her voice on the other end of the line was like a balm to my soul – she was my rock, and talking to her helped me to see that I did have options, and that I wasn't as powerless as I thought I was. Tricia helped me to slowly build up the courage I needed to leave Charlie, and she helped me to see that there was at least one person out there who cared for me.

I often wondered if her psychic abilities allowed her to pick up on the truth, but if they did she never said. Tricia became something of a lifeline to me.

On one particular day, I was on the phone to her and she was begging me to leave Charlie, as she had done on so many occasions.

By now we were chatting regularly on the phone but usually it was me calling her in tears after another outburst from Charlie.

'You can do it, Tina,' she said. 'I know you can. Just go. Take the kids and go!'

'I can't,' I wept. 'It's not as simple as that.'

'Yes it is,' she urged. 'You must go to a refuge and get away from Charlie. Just leave him.'

I didn't know what a refuge even was, let alone how to find one, and over and over again I told Tricia I wasn't strong enough.

But then, something happened.

After the phone call, I sat there on my bed, weeping despondently – suddenly I heard a noise. Alex was hovering in the doorway.

I looked up, sopping wet tissues balled into my hand, my eyes still red with crying, but I didn't know what to say to him.

He walked slowly to the bed, climbed up next to me and wrapped his small arms around my thick shoulders.

'Don't worry, Mum,' he whispered softly. 'It'll be okay.'

And with that I wept even harder. But then I opened up my arms and for the first time, I held my eldest son in a loving embrace.

It was the first time he'd ever come up to me and given me a hug and it made me feel so guilty.

I'd had so many thoughts of suicide yet it was my child who was telling me everything would be okay.

'*They deserve so much better than this*,' I thought angrily. '*They don't have to grow up in this poisonous household. It's ruined my life already – I won't let it ruin theirs too.*'

At that moment I knew there was something strong inside of me, somewhere beneath all the hurt and pain. I felt for the first time that one day, I could be the mother they really needed and deserved. And there was only one way that was going to happen.

Two days later, I stood in my bedroom, looking down at my bags, steeling myself to pick them up and walk out.

Half an hour before, Charlie had slammed out of the house as usual, but I'd woken up that morning feeling somehow different from usual.

Thomas was now eighteen months old and I'd had just about as much as I could take of Charlie's constant abuse and sex demands. I hated him with every fibre of my being.

He'd demanded sex the night before, as usual, but I couldn't bear it any longer and had tried to push him away. Then, he'd thrown himself on top of me, pinned me to the bed with all his strength and forced himself inside me.

But instead of crying that night, I just lay there, frozen to the mattress, resolving not to take one more minute of this abuse.

And the next day, after he'd left I'd raced upstairs, grabbed handfuls of clothes for me and the kids and stuffed them into every bag I could find. I also packed Tom's blue folder – if I was going, then he was coming with me.

But now I stood looking down at the bags overflowing with clothes, breathing hard after the frenzy of activity and wondering – could I really do this?

Suddenly, Daniel wandered in.

'Are you going?' he asked.

And suddenly my strength returned: 'Yes, I'm going,' I said, heaving my bags off the bed.

Then I pulled my shoulders back, ran my hands through my ponytail and looked at him – did he want to come too?

I didn't really expect him to say yes as he was so close to Charlie, but even so, I had to ask.

'Nah, I'm all right here with Dad,' he said. 'But I'll help you with the bags.'

I was surprised – Daniel had a strong bond with his dad and I thought that he would side with him, but actually, he was really helpful with getting all the kids bundled into their coats then we lugged all the stuff to my sister's house fifteen minutes away.

She was the only person I knew in the area – I couldn't think of anywhere else to go.

And when I rang her bell that morning, I felt a huge sense of fear and relief wash over me at the same time. '*I've done it*,' I thought, '*after sixteen years of abuse, I've done it. I've left him*.' I was a grown woman and this was the first time I'd had enough courage to walk out the door. It might have sounded easy, but it was one of the hardest things I've ever done. I had no money, no place to live, and since the age of nine I had spent my life in fear of Charlie.

Lisa opened the door and stood staring at us all there on her doorstep for a few seconds before I started sobbing.

'I've left him, Lisa,' I wept. 'I can't do it any more. I can't go back and I didn't know where else to go.'

In an instant she threw her arms around me: 'Hey, hey,' she soothed. 'It's okay. You can stay here. I won't let anything happen to you.'

So we trundled in – me, Alex, Tammy and Thomas – and Lisa showed us to the back room where we dumped all our stuff. Then we all went into the living room and while the kids played, me and Lisa talked. The time seemed to pass so slowly that day and I walked around, numb with fear and shock at what I'd just done.

It felt great to not be near Charlie, but all day long I was watching the clock. The closer it got to five, the more scared I became. And I started panicking.

'He's going to know where I am,' I said to Lisa. 'He's going to find me, he's going to turn up at the house. I know he is!'

'Don't worry,' she said. 'You're not going back to him. It doesn't matter if he turns up, we'll deal with it.'

As I sat there on the settee and saw the minute hand tick over to 5 p.m., my stomach began to churn and I felt the fear rise up in my throat. But then nothing happened. Every few minutes I kept glancing at the clock – but it turned six and still nobody had turned up.

I was waiting and waiting for something to happen.

Finally, it got to 7 p.m. and my sister said, 'Come on, we'll put the kids to bed in the back room.'

So for a while we distracted ourselves getting the kids ready for bed, laying down some mattresses in her back room and within half an hour they were all asleep.

'You deserve a drink!' Lisa announced as I trailed her back to the kitchen. 'It's been a big day.'

So she opened the fridge, took out a bottle of Lambrini and we sat drinking it in the living room. By now her boyfriend Dave had come home and was upstairs in the bedroom on the computer while we chatted in the living room.

Then, all of a sudden there was a loud bang on the door, and my stomach dropped through the floor.

Lisa and I both looked at each other, then she started to get up.

'No!' I whispered urgently. 'Don't open the door! Don't answer it. Just leave it.'

But then the bang came again and Lisa stood up.

'Look, don't worry,' she told me. 'You stay in here, don't come out, just stay sat down. I'll go and answer the door.'

But as soon as she'd turned the handle, Charlie came crashing into the house.

'Where the fuck is she?' he bellowed.

He tried to barge his way past Lisa but she pushed him back – yet still he kept shouting, 'Where is she? Get her in the bloody car. She's coming back with me now. Where are the kids?'

'She's not coming with you,' my sister yelled back. 'You're not taking the kids – just leave them where they are and get out of the house!'

I was peeping through the door hinge to see what was going on and at that moment Charlie raised his fist to Lisa, just as Dave came running down the stairs.

'Move the fuck out of the way!' Charlie yelled.

'You hit her and I'll punch your lights out!' Dave warned him.

I'd had enough. I couldn't bear to see any more. I'd dragged these innocent people into my mess and I wouldn't let anyone get hurt for my sake. So I walked into the hallway, shaking more than I'd ever done in my life, and spoke to Charlie, 'I'm not coming back. I'm staying. Leave me alone.'

It was the first time I'd ever stood up to him and my whole body felt like it had turned to jelly but I was determined.

At that moment, Charlie pushed my sister aside and came at me.

'Get in the car now!' he spat in my face, so close I could smell the rancid alcohol on his breath. 'You're coming back with me.'

'I'm not,' I replied, standing my ground.

I flinched then, thinking he was going to hit me for defying him. But instead he just stood there, and for a single moment, I thought it was all going to be over.

But then he turned away, and took a swipe at my glass of Lambrini, which smashed all over the floor. 'Where are the kids? I'm taking them now.'

My sister was next to me now. 'You're not taking the kids. They're fast asleep, leave them. Come back in the morning and talk.'

But he ignored her – instead he walked into the backroom and one by one, picked up the children and took them out to the car. They'd all been fast asleep until now but as the horrible scene unfolded and they were lifted out of their slumber and flung into the car, they started bawling.

He then came back in and tried to drag me out of the house by my arm.

I squirmed and wriggled out of his grip then I picked up the only thing that I could see, Tom's blue folder, and I ran out of the house with it.

I passed the kids all crying in the car and fled up the street but Charlie ran after me, grabbed my arm and slapped me across the face.

'Get in that car now! You're going nowhere!'

He had hold of my arm still and was dragging me down the road. I saw my kids in the car, looked at their crying faces and all the fight evaporated out of me. I realised he was right, I wasn't going anywhere that night.

Where was I going to go in the middle of the night without my kids? Suddenly, I felt so stupid. Whenever I'd thought about leaving Charlie in my head, I'd never escaped. He always found me. Now, it had become a reality.

So I ended up getting in the car and he drove me home. When we got in the door he shouted to the kids, 'Get up the stairs and get in bed.'

Then he turned around and locked the front door behind us and put the keys in his trousers, so I couldn't leave. Then he turned to me: 'Get in bed and get to fucking sleep.'

I sat on the bed that night, crying my eyes out while Charlie watched TV downstairs. I had almost done it, I had almost managed to leave him, but he had dragged me back into his stinking life. Was I ever going to get away from him?

Chapter 16

...Gone!

My first attempt at escape had failed but something had changed inside me and the more time passed, the stronger I felt. Tricia's friendship and her unswerving belief in me were finally getting through and as time went on, the more I yearned for escape.

I wanted to feel what it was like to have a normal life. My sister had a partner and they were happy and had kids. I wanted that! I wanted to see what it was like to be in a relationship, to be loved, to love somebody. I used to daydream of what it might be like to be happy, instead of stuck in this monstrous situation.

Sometimes, after a busy day cooking, cleaning and looking after the kids I'd find myself stopping in the middle of the living room, with the vacuum still on, struck by the thought that I could be doing this for ever.

Then I'd be gripped with panic.

'*I'll be an old woman before I escape!*' I'd be screaming inside my head. '*I'm never going to feel what it's like to have a normal life, to be able to live on my own, have my own house, and do my own things. I'm never going to know what it's like to be happy.*'

I really thought that I'd never have anything that other people took for granted. I'd never even had the chance to walk down the street and talk to people or go out shopping with my own money to buy what I wanted, when I wanted. I wanted the responsibility of paying my own bills and making my own way in the world. I'd been trapped under my stepfather's roof for sixteen long years, trapped in his warped and abusive world and now I wanted out.

Sometimes I'd look at him asleep, his mouth hanging open, his sour breath filling the room and I'd think, '*Yes, I could do ten years for murder. Why not?*' I could not imagine that prison could be any worse than the one I had been trapped in for sixteen years.

I hated being near him. I hated everything about him and he still demanded sex of me every night. Now, he even told to me 'to look like I was enjoying it' so I'd lie there with a fake smile plastered all over my face. I'd had enough.

I suppose I could have got a knife and stabbed him – or drugged his drink and then suffocated him. But then, what would happen to the kids? They'd have to go into care. No, I couldn't kill him because then they would be alone in this world and that wouldn't be fair.

But every day, I felt his control over me slipping away and slowly, I found my own voice.

One day, he asked me where he'd left his keys and I just told him to find them himself.

I hardly knew what I was saying until it came out of me, and I feared he'd come back with a slap, but nothing happened.

Then, a few days later he said he couldn't work the computer and I said, 'Oh, what a surprise!'

Again, nothing happened. They were only small, sarcastic little digs but there were no repercussions from them. I felt something changing in our relationship. The balance of power was shifting and I was getting stronger.

Then, I did it. I left him – and still to this day, I don't know where I found the strength.

It was six months after my first aborted escape and two days after Christmas.

It had been a tough day, but no different than the usual. My resentment had been building ever since I had tried to leave him the first time, and the numb, dead feelings that I had had for many years had been replaced by anger and hate. My courage was building up too – and I could feel Charlie's hold over me getting weaker and weaker.

Charlie had been having a go at me all day and by eight that evening I exploded. This was it – I wasn't going to take it any more.

Upstairs in the bedroom, I told him straight. 'I've had enough. I want you to leave me alone. I want my own life,' I said firmly.

Charlie looked like he'd been hit by a bus, and suddenly I glimpsed weakness and vulnerability pass over his face.

'You're not leaving me,' he insisted. 'I'll kill myself before you leave me!'

I was taken aback – this was something new. Did he honestly think he was going to persuade me to stay through emotional blackmail? I *wanted* him dead!

But then it hit me – Charlie thought I loved him! He honestly believed that I cared for him, otherwise how could he imagine such a threat would work? It astounded me – after all, he'd seen me cry myself to sleep every night. It seemed amazing that he could have so little understanding of another person's feelings.

Well, if he was going to try that tack, I'd play him at his own game.

'No, you won't,' I replied nonchalantly. 'You won't do it.'

'Yeah?' he said defiantly. 'Just watch me!'

So I sat there, bemused, as he went to the medicine cabinet and came back with two packets of painkillers. He had a tumbler of whisky and he opened the first packet and downed it at once on the bed in front of me.

'*What a load of nonsense!*' I thought to myself. '*He's never going to go through with it.*'

'Look!' he said, gulping down the pills. 'I'm doing it. I'll be dead in the morning.'

I just sat staring from the other side of the bed,

trying to look as bored as possible, but all the while thinking, '*Is he serious?*'

When he saw his little show hadn't impressed me, he took some more. I knew it wasn't enough to kill him.

'It's happening,' he said. 'It's going to work. I can feel it. I'm going.'

I watched him intently as his eyes became heavier and heavier – after half an hour he passed out.

There was no sex that night, which was great, and no playing with him either, which was also great.

I just lay there watching him till three in the morning. And as I lay there next to him that night, I started planning what I'd do if he did die one day.

I thought, '*I'd get up and just leave. And I would not even ring anyone to tell them he was dead. I'd just leave him there.*'

The next day, Charlie woke up at seven with a banging headache.

I opened my eyes to see him holding his head in his hands and leaning over the side of the bed, in obvious agony.

'I see it didn't work then,' I said drily before getting up to go to the bathroom.

Yes, something had definitely changed between us and with every hour that passed, I felt stronger and stronger.

*

So when, later in the day, I was sitting at the computer and Charlie ordered me to get the house spotless, I simply ignored him.

'This floor needs to be cleaned now!' he yelled again.

He was obviously embarrassed and annoyed about his dramatics the night before – and I'm sure the headache wasn't helping.

But I just shot him a withering look and said, 'Well, go on then. You know where the vacuum is.'

He stomped off, grabbed the vacuum and threw it on the floor in front of me like a sulky schoolkid. But I just carried on at the computer as if nothing had happened.

He could see he wasn't getting to me any more and he didn't like it.

So he came round the side of the computer, turned it off and took out all the plugs.

I got up with an exaggerated yawn, plonked myself on the settee then flicked on the telly – and I didn't touch the floor, the vacuum or anything else for the rest of the day.

Inside I was still scared, still waiting for the beating, but it never came.

A few hours later, I was on the phone to Tricia.

'Something's changed,' I said. 'I don't know what it is. Maybe it's because I've never stood up to him before. I don't understand it. Is it because I'm older? I don't know.'

'I don't know either, honey, but I do know one thing. You can leave him now. It's going to be okay.'

Two days later I'd made up my mind.

At around mid-morning I confronted him, bolstered by a strength I'd never felt before.

'Right, that's it,' I said. 'I'm going. I've had enough.'

Charlie started to crumble before my eyes – he seemed like a desperate man and actually begged me not to leave.

'Don't go, please,' he said. 'Just give it a month. If after a month then you want out, I'll let you go. I love you. Please don't leave.'

I didn't know what to do – I'd never been in this situation before. Was Charlie really saying that if I stayed for the month then he'd let me go with his full permission and everything would be okay? It seemed too good to be true. I thought, '*Yes, I can do this. I can do four more weeks and then I'd be out of here for ever.*'

'All right, I said. 'Four more weeks and then I'm gone.'

At that point he took a permanent marker from the drawer, went upstairs to our bedroom and ten minutes later, when I went up to retrieve a jumper from my drawers, I was met with the most extraordinary sight.

He'd written: '*Tina, I love you*' in large, scrawly

letters over one wall, then above our bed he'd penned our names and circled them with a big love heart.

I felt sick.

'Let's go out for dinner,' he said to me the next day, New Year's Eve.

He was trying to turn on the charm and hadn't even shouted at me all day.

But my mind was made up and I realised something – what had I been thinking? I wasn't going to wait a month until I left him. It was the beginning of a new year, and I deserved a new start. Forget waiting another four weeks – I was leaving and nothing he could do or say was going to change that.

'No, I don't want to go,' I said. 'I don't want anything from you. I'm leaving.'

He glowered at me then walked out of the house and half an hour later he returned with a tin of white paint, went upstairs again and painted over all the writing he'd done on our walls the day before.

When I saw it, I nearly started laughing – instead of painting the whole wall, he'd just gone over the black marker with the white paint. So against our grey walls, you could still see what he'd written only now it was bright white paint!

I knew I had to go and if he didn't like it, then tough. If he tried to do anything to me then I'd take it, because now I was determined – I was either going to leave that house or die trying. I didn't care one way or another. Maybe he would kill me, but it was a risk I was going to take.

So the following morning – New Year's Day – I told Charlie once and for all that I couldn't stay for another month and I was leaving.

He just sat there on the bed, looking dazed and broken, his shoulders hunched over in resignation.

I started packing my bags again, getting everything I'd need for me and the kids. And then the strangest thing happened – Charlie started to cry! It was only the second time I'd seen him cry in my life and I suddenly felt as if I held all the cards. I was the strong one, I was leaving and he wasn't going to do anything about it!

'Don't go,' he begged through his tears. 'Please don't go.'

'I'm going, Charlie – you can't stop me.'

And then everything changed again and his misery turned to anger.

'Well, you're not taking the kids.'

'I am!'

'You can take *one* of them.'

And then *I* burst out crying. In a second I had lost all the control and he was in charge again. I didn't know what to do. He always managed to find my weakest spot.

I feared Charlie's anger – if I tried to take them all

with me, he might attack us. So now I had to choose one of my children.

It was the hardest decision of my life.

I really wanted to take Tammy with me but by now she was having injections into her tummy every day as medication, which Charlie and I had been trained to do using sterile gloves. She had so many medications and equipment for her condition, her room resembled a hospital. Everything was there for her – the house was specially adapted for her – how could I take her with me? I didn't even know where I was going, let alone if it would be suitable for her.

As for Alex, he was the eldest and the best equipped to survive without me.

So I made the heartbreaking decision to leave the two kids, and take Thomas. After all, he was just a baby and I was still breastfeeding.

I packed up all the stuff I could carry and walked out of that house at midday on 1 January. It was horrible. Both Tammy and Alex were crying – they wanted to come and couldn't understand why I was leaving them.

'Look, it'll be okay,' I tried to reassure them as I hugged them both close to me. 'You'll still see me.'

At that moment, I didn't know if what I was saying was true, I had no way of knowing how Charlie would react, but I was hoping he'd still let them see me. Looking at their tear-streaked faces, I was overwhelmed by guilt. But more than anything, I knew then how much I loved them. In all that time, I'd never bonded properly with Alex and I'd found it harder and harder to show the children love and affection. Only now, when I had to leave them, I knew deep down that I loved them more than anything, even if I had trouble showing it.

'Come on,' said Charlie. 'You can use the car to take the stuff up to your sister's.'

It surprised me that he would help me to go to my sister's, but then, everything about him had been a surprise that day. He had crumbled in front of me, which I didn't expect. So I loaded what I could into the car then he dropped me back at Lisa's.

'I'll give you two years,' he announced as I opened the car door. 'Within two years you'll be back here with me.'

'No, I won't,' I said shaking my head.

'You will,' he sneered. 'Because nobody will want you. Nobody will have you. You'll be back living with me within two years. Guaranteed.'

Then he slammed the door and drove off.

I sat on the settee that night and cried in my sister's arms. For the first time I was on my own and I was scared. I think I was in shock. For all those years, my warped mind had been convinced that I could never escape. I'd been kept a prisoner by Charlie's mental torture. And now I'd proved that wrong. What was I going to do? How was I going to survive?

Lisa helped to wipe away my tears and then got up and smiled at me. 'You did it, Tina. I'm really proud of you. Now, come on, let's get something to eat.'

Lisa shoved a take-away menu in my hand.

'What do you want?' she asked casually as she went searching through the mess in her living room to find the cordless phone.

The words and numbers swam before my eyes.

What did I want? I didn't know! Nobody had ever asked me what I wanted before and my mind was a total blank.

I panicked. '*What do I say? I'm twenty-six and I've never had to think what I wanted to eat before now because I've always been told.*'

'I, uh…I don't know.'

'Well, come on,' she snapped. 'We're all hungry. Just pick something.'

'All right, I'll have a cheese and tomato pizza.'

It was the first thing that popped into my mind!

Later, I got Thomas settled next to me on a mattress on the floor in the spare room upstairs and watched him as he slept soundly by the tangerine light of the street lamps.

And then I started crying. And I cried and cried and cried.

'*What am I doing?*' I thought.

I'd dreamt my whole life of that day, that day when I would be free and yet now that it was here I was so unbelievably frightened.

I didn't feel free. I still felt controlled, still felt ashamed, and still felt afraid – of everything. I didn't know how I was going to cope. I'd left my kids there with him.

Now, what was I going to do with my life?

Chapter 17
A New Start

That first night of freedom, I cried myself to sleep. But that morning I woke up for the first time in years without Charlie. It was wonderful.

Just as quickly, my elation was replaced by a tornado of emotions – fear, sadness, loneliness and guilt. Yet underneath it all I felt a real sense of excitement. My life was about to begin and who knew where it would take me?

I called Tricia right away.

'See, I told you, you could do it,' she said. 'I knew it all along.'

'Yeah, but I don't know how I did it,' I said, still in shock at leaving Charlie after all these years. 'For so long, it felt impossible, but in the end, it was easy. So easy.'

'You had to wait for the right time, sweetie,' she said. 'And now's the right time.'

I woke up Thomas and we walked downstairs together and suddenly I realised how untidy and cluttered Lisa's house was. My place was always spotless because I was constantly cleaning, but Lisa didn't have my over-zealous standards and there were a few old plates and cups that needed washing, boxes of old take-aways piled high in the kitchen. It wasn't that bad really, but Charlie had made me neurotic about cleanliness.

'I can't stay here,' I said to Lisa over my mug of tea that morning. 'I need to make a proper start in my life and I can't do that here.'

'You can stay as long as you need to,' she replied. 'But, listen, why don't you ring social services and see what they can do?'

So I called social services that morning and told them I'd just left my abusive partner and I had a child with me and nowhere to live. They gave me the number of Women's Aid so I called them and explained my situation to them.

I still couldn't tell the truth about Charlie being my stepfather – how could I just come out with it? How do you even start a conversation like that?

For so long I'd had the threat hanging over me that if I ever told anyone I'd be dead that I was still scared. Plus, of course, he had my kids. If I told someone, I'd be putting them at risk.

They said they could put me in a refuge and we arranged to meet at their support centre in town later that day.

'Now, what about money?' Lisa asked next.

'I've got a bank account where they put in my benefits but I can't get into it and Charlie has his name on the account so he takes it all.'

'Right,' said Lisa. 'We'll go and sort that out then, shall we?'

So Lisa took me into town and we went to the bank to take Charlie's name off the account and to order a bank card for me. I'd never had one before.

Then I withdrew a hundred pounds from the cashier's till.

It felt amazing – for the first time I had my own money in my hand and I could go out and spend it on whatever I wanted!

The brief exhilaration was quickly followed by a sense of guilt and fear. I thought I would have to answer for this. I felt like I was going to get caught by Charlie and sent back to live in his house.

'Relax,' my sister sighed as I glanced over my shoulder for about the hundredth time that day. I kept thinking he was there, following me, watching everything I was doing.

'He's not there and he's not coming to get you so just chill out!'

But I just couldn't relax. For one thing, it was all so new to me. I had my freedom at last but I had no idea what to do with it!

It was like putting a six-year-old in the street to survive on her own. Most people teach a child so that when they get older and they live on their own they can be independent. But when you've never been taught that and all of sudden you're a twenty-six-year-old woman who's never made a decision for herself, having to get by on your own, it's terrifying.

Even though I was used to doing things round the house, I'd always been told what to do, how and when to do it. Thinking for myself was an entirely new experience and it's something I had to get used to. Fast.

Walking into the support centre run by Women's Aid, I was greeted by a small, lithe woman in her forties with an auburn bob and a warm smile.

'Hi there,' she extended her hand towards me. 'Pleased to meet you. I'm Jennifer, a support worker. Why don't you take a seat?'

I was so nervous and upset – talking to people for the first time about Charlie was awful. I felt so stupid for staying with him for so long and I thought everyone would blame me, say it was my fault for sticking with him.

And of course I was back to lying again because I wasn't ready to tell people he was my stepfather so when they started asking questions like how long we'd been together, I had to make up some false dates.

But Jennifer was really lovely and supportive and tried to make me feel at ease, pouring me cups of tea and offering tissues whenever I started to cry.

'Listen, you'll be fine,' she said reassuringly. 'We'll put you in a refuge where he can't find you. There's one ten miles away which has some space.'

'No, I can't go that far away,' I said. 'My kids are here and I want to be able to see them.'

So they agreed to put me in a refuge closer to home and within an hour we were on our way there in Jennifer's car.

I was pleasantly surprised when we got there to find it was a block of six little houses, facing each other in rows of two, all surrounded by a wooden fence. It looked lovely, really homely.

I was shown into my own two-bedroomed house, which was already fully furnished and found it was very nice and clean.

The other houses were occupied by other women and then two of the houses were reserved for staff.

Jennifer gave me a run-down of the rules: we weren't allowed alcohol on the premises, we had to leave contact numbers of where we were if we stayed out at weekends, we paid twenty pounds a week for rent, ten pounds for gas and electricity and ten pounds went into a deposit against breakages. There were inspections once a week and courses and groups we had to attend all week long.

I didn't mind all the rules, it made me feel safe and, after all, I was used to being told what to do.

*

In truth, I loved living in the refuge. I was assigned a key worker who came and spoke to me once a week to find out how I was getting on. And there were plenty of opportunities to meet other women in the same situation.

Every Friday they held a breakfast 'meet and greet' – during the week they'd come round and ask if you wanted a fry up or continental, then on Friday mornings they'd lay out a big table in one of the staff houses for everyone to come and chat over breakfast.

On Wednesday they held a coffee morning at the support centre in town. It was a chance to meet not just the people in the refuge but those who worked with Women's Aid. Everyone there had been through an experience of domestic abuse so people understood and we were all in the same boat. Most of us brought our kids along too so there were plenty of children for Thomas to play with.

We even had cooking lessons and I learned how to make cheese and sweetcorn samosas, which were beautiful!

Over time I started to learn how to organise my life on my own. It felt very strange not having someone tell me what to do. On the first day, I asked my key worker what time I should cook tea and she looked at me kindly and simply said, 'You can cook when you want to, Tina. It's up to you.'

I felt like I was a blank piece of paper without any instructions. For the first time I had to write out a plan for my life and do it all myself. It was really difficult but I was starting to enjoy it.

I'd never really cooked very well before then because Charlie always wanted something you could just bung in the oven, like chips, or something you could heat up in the microwave, like beans. So making food from scratch was also a challenge and I was forever setting off the fire alarm!

Being in the refuge gave me a sense of security, which I desperately needed. They were very strict about keeping the location secret so if we went shopping in town we always had to get the taxi to drop us back at the end of the road, round the corner and walk the rest of the way. And all our post was sent to a PO Box number, which the support centre then picked up and distributed to the women staying in the refuge.

I'd been there for three weeks when I got a call on my mobile from Charlie.

'The kids want to see you,' he said in a voice stripped of emotion.

It was horrible to have to talk to Charlie but at the same time I was so happy to know the children wanted to see me. I'd been desperate to see them too but I didn't know how to approach Charlie to ask for contact.

I'd also been feeling really guilty – as Thomas and I enjoyed ourselves in our new home, all I could think about at night were the kids I'd left, stuck in that house with Charlie.

We arranged to meet at a pub in town where Charlie treated us all to lunch. He was trying to be nice to me, for the first time in my life, in the false hope that I'd realise what I was missing and come home.

Seeing the kids again was heartbreaking.

'We miss you, Mum,' Tammy wept in my arms.

Later that day, I went outside to the playground with Alex and Tammy.

Alex was pushing himself backwards and forwards on the swings when he said to me, 'Dad told me to tell you he wants you to come home.'

I felt for the poor boy. Charlie was now using him to try and get messages to me, using Alex as his go-between. It wasn't fair on him, he was only eleven years old.

'I can't, love. I'm sorry,' I said. 'I don't want to be with him any more.'

Neither of them was really old enough to understand, and how could they? They had no idea of the extent of Charlie's abuse.

At the end of the afternoon I went to catch the bus back to the refuge. Charlie wanted to give me a lift but I couldn't let him know where I was living.

'You'll be with me in two years, guaranteed,' he said at the bus stop, just like the last time. 'I'll have you back.'

'No. You won't,' I responded, more confident now than the last time. I'd been living on my own for three weeks and was managing quite happily without him. 'I want to be able to live on my own. I want to meet other people.'

'Nobody will have you. Who'd want you? Look at the state of you. Look at you! You're a disgrace, just like your mum.'

It was the way Charlie had always tried to control me, by putting me down and eating away at my self-esteem. Except now I was going to the classes at the support centre, I knew that it was a common tactic by abusive partners. And the reason? It worked! For a long time after I left Charlie, my confidence was at rock bottom. When I went out and saw men walking along the street and they looked at me, I put my head down. '*Who'd want me?*' I thought. '*I'm a fat, ugly mess.*' Even if they did want to be with me, I reasoned, they'd probably make my life miserable, just like Charlie. To me, every man was a potential rapist and abuser – I simply couldn't trust them.

Two months after moving into the refuge, my sister called. 'Do you fancy coming out on a night out?'

'What? I've never been on a proper night out in my life!' I laughed back at her. 'How on earth am I supposed to go out? I've got a baby.'

'It's all right,' she said. 'I've got a babysitter for

next Saturday. Bring Thomas to the house and she'll look after him too.'

It was so exciting – a night out! I looked forward to it all week and before I left I told the refuge I was going to stay at my sister's and left all my contact details so they could reach me in an emergency.

Saturday morning came and I packed up mine and Thomas' things and got the bus to Lisa's. But as soon as I walked in, she grabbed me by the arm, wheeled me around and marched me straight out of the door again.

'We're going shopping!' she trilled brightly.

It was my first time clothes shopping for myself without Charlie telling me what to buy, and as much as I would have liked to enjoy it, I was really nervous the whole time.

Whenever I was out, I was scared of bumping into Charlie so while Lisa manoeuvred me in and out of shops, expertly picking out tops and matching them to skirts, trousers and shoes, I was a bundle of nerves, hardly concentrating on what was going on.

Eventually I managed to find a nice, low-cut black top and a pair of black trousers with a black jacket.

'It's not Halloween!' my sister teased.

'Black's flattering!' I retorted.

Later that evening, as I twirled in the living room for Lisa and her boyfriend Dave, they both complimented me, telling me I looked really nice.

But I didn't feel it – I'd been put down for so long, I didn't have any confidence in my looks.

We left the kids with the babysitter, took some money out of the cashpoint and headed for the first pub of the night – me, Lisa, Dave and his sister Sophie.

We parked ourselves at a table in the corner while Dave went to the bar to get the first round – blue WKDs. I'd never had them before but they were really sweet and delicious.

The first round disappeared within half an hour and soon we were all getting up to take turns at the bar – we had five rounds in total at the pub. And, by that point Sophie and Lisa were really tipsy and giggly.

But I didn't feel a thing.

I was drinking these WKDs like water, yet they had no effect on me whatsoever. Everyone was chatting away, getting drunk, laughing and enjoying the night, but I felt myself becoming more and more withdrawn.

I didn't know how to act or what to do – it was all so new to me. I couldn't relax.

'Hey,' Lisa leaned in to me, her eyes trained on a dark-haired man in his mid-thirties nursing a pint at the bar. 'That guy there's looking at you.'

'Oh no, don't be silly,' I squirmed, sneaking a quick peek then turning quickly away.

'Why don't you go and talk to him?' she said.

'No, I really can't,' I said. I wasn't ready for any - thing like that yet.

After our fifth round, Dave announced we should visit another pub, where we stayed for a round, then he corralled us all to go to a nightclub.

By the time we got there I'd lost count of the number of drinks I'd had but still, I felt stone cold sober. The only noticeable effect was a constant need to visit the ladies!

Walking into the nightclub was so strange – the loud music, the people dancing – I felt like I didn't belong. The only other time I'd been to a nightclub was when I was fourteen but now I was old enough to be there and it didn't feel right at all.

I needed to start enjoying myself!

So I walked straight up to the bar and asked for a triple vodka and Coke. The bartender handed me a massive glass and I knocked it back in one go.

God in heaven – it felt like my mouth was on fire! But it did the trick. I started to lose the fear that had gripped me all night and I could feel myself relaxing and soaking up the atmosphere.

Back out in the cold night air, we staggered to the next club. My sister linked her arm into mine and we lurched down the street, singing and swaying from side to side.

For the first time in my life I was having a good time!

At the next place, Dave ordered After Shock liqueurs and we all stood at the bar, shouting, 'One Two Three,' before downing the shots.

By now I was really drunk and headed onto the dance floor to enjoy a boogie. Meanwhile, Lisa went to talk to Dave outside and handed me her bottle of WKD to hold.

So I was dancing, holding her drink and mine and getting really confused about which was mine – by the time she came back in, I'd drunk both! So she went up to the bar to get us more drinks, came back, handed them to me and the whole thing started all over again!

I don't know long I'd been dancing before Sophie and I went to the loos – time was moving in really strange ways and I was losing track of all the drinks I had on the go.

'Can I borrow your phone?' she slurred as I tried to focus long enough to reapply my lipstick in the mirror. 'I need to text my boyfriend. We had a row but I want to make things up and my battery's dead.'

'Course you can, Sophie lovely,' I burbled. By now I was totally smashed out of my face!

She was trying to send a text message to her bloke but we were so drunk we couldn't work out where the number one was on the phone!

'Where is it?' I giggled stupidly. 'Where's the bloody one gone?'

It was so funny, I nearly peed myself!

Then my sister came in and looked upset. She started crying, then I started crying and then Sophie started crying too. We were all stood there in this toilet crying and none of us knew why! But that night even crying was fun – at twenty-six years of age I felt like the teenager I had never been.

Flash forward and I was back on the dance floor, where Dave's mate Kevin was trying to get close enough to dance with me.

He must have liked me but I thought he was ugly as hell so I kept bopping behind my sister so he wasn't able to get near.

Still, when he offered to buy me a drink, I didn't refuse. It was a free drink after all! I was having a great time, it felt amazing. Not once did I ever think about Charlie or care about him or care about what had gone on. I was free!

The next thing I was lying flat on my back after tripping up on the dance floor, and I was laughing so hard I couldn't get up.

Kevin put his hand down to help me up and as he pulled me to my feet, he planted a big smacker on my mouth. Oh my God, I wanted to be sick right there.

Maybe it was the drink, or maybe I just wasn't ready to be intimate with someone, but mostly I think it was because Kevin really wasn't my type.

Either way, I'd had enough and told Lisa I was ready to head home. It was four in the morning by the time the taxi dropped us back at her place and I vaguely remember climbing up the stairs on my hands and knees to get into the bed in the spare room before I passed out.

I woke up at ten to the sound of a text message beeping on my phone.

Jesus! I'd never known what a hangover was like until that moment and, oh Lord, it really was bad.

My head felt like it was going to explode, my vision was blurred and I could still taste the After Shocks in my mouth, which instantly sent a wave of nausea through my body.

I just wanted to sleep but the phone had woken me and I wondered who it could be – maybe it was the refuge?

The letters swam before my eyes as I tried to make sense of the words. It was from Charlie.

'*So, does this mean you love me?*' it read. '*Are you going to come home now?*'

WHAT? What the hell was this all about?

Then another text came through. '*You sent me this last night,*' it read. And below was a long mushy text saying I loved and missed him and I wanted to come home.

I was sure I didn't send anything to Charlie the night before. And I never would have said anything like that. I was drunk, yes, but not mad!

Then I remembered – Sophie's text! We hadn't been able to work the phone because we were so drunk and it must have been sent to Charlie instead of her boyfriend.

I let out a pitiful groan and rolled onto my back.

Then I quickly typed out the message. '*This wasn't from me. A friend used my phone last night to text her boyfriend but it got sent to you by mistake. It's not from me and I'm not coming home.*'

As soon as I pressed send, I let out a sigh of relief.

A message quickly popped back into my inbox: '*OH RIGHT!*'

Was he angry? Who cares? And anyway, I couldn't worry about that now, I had a little boy waiting for me downstairs and a cracking hangover to contend with.

I delicately pulled myself out of bed then crept downstairs, fearing any movement might send me flying to the loo.

Lisa and Dave were already up and I told them about the text message mix up. They couldn't stop laughing. Then they reminded me of the kiss with Kevin and I really did think I was going to throw up.

Soon the kids were wandering in demanding toast and somehow we managed to rustle up some breakfast then spent the rest of the day nursing our hangovers on the sofa and watching telly.

All in all it had been a fantastic evening, my first proper night out and it gave me a huge lift to think there might be more to come.

But I had a hangover for three days straight and to this day I can't drink the shots we did that night.

Chapter 18

On My Own

In March, Jennifer, my support worker, came up to me in the support centre to tell me she'd made an appointment for a solicitor to visit me in the refuge. I'd told her how much I missed the older kids and wanted to get them back and she said she'd help me to go through the legal channels. I was excited the day the solicitor Beth turned up, and after I'd made her a cup of tea we went to sit in the living room together. However, after we went over my initial details, the questions started to get harder and harder.

'How long have you been with Charlie?' she asked.

'Erm, I don't know,' I replied. I couldn't tell her the truth or she'd know I was just a young girl when it all started.

Then she asked me why Charlie and I had the same surname, Jenkins, if we weren't married. I didn't know what to say.

Next she asked me why Charlie's name wasn't on any of the kids' birth certificates. I just said I didn't know again.

I couldn't answer half her questions and in the end, it struck me that if I pursued Charlie for custody of the children, the truth would have to come out and I wasn't ready for that. It was too much, too soon. Leaving Charlie had been massive for me, and I wasn't ready, mentally, physically or emotionally, for this at the moment.

So after a few more questions, I stopped Beth.

'Look, I don't think I'm going to go for custody.'

'Really?' She was very surprised. 'Why?'

'Well, I don't think I'm ready yet,' I said. 'I'm not settled. I don't think it's a good idea.'

It was heartbreaking but I didn't know any other way. I wanted to tell her everything but I believed that Charlie would kill me – and it frightened me to think about what would happen to the kids. I may have escaped him physically, but emotionally in so many ways his claws were dug deep into me.

It took me right back to that time all those years ago when the social workers turned up at the house; he'd kept me quiet then and he was still keeping me quiet now. Even though I'd got away from him, he still had all the control.

Meanwhile, Charlie had somehow found out where I lived.

One Friday afternoon I went shopping in town with one of the other residents from the refuge. We'd walked down the long hill which took us to Morrison's in the town centre then she left to do her own thing and later I got a taxi home, making the driver drop me off round the corner as usual.

An hour later, I got a knock on my door – it was Jennifer.

'Charlie knows where you are,' she said solemnly. 'He's been caught on CCTV outside the refuge. He must have followed you home.'

Jennifer knew what Charlie's car looked like because he'd already been caught patrolling up and down outside the support centre in town, but now he'd tracked me down to the refuge.

My heart started racing. I was frightened he would come and drag me away.

The next day, I got a text message from Charlie, saying he needed to talk to me about the kids.

'*You followed me yesterday*,' I wrote back. '*You know where I am.*'

He didn't even try to deny it.

I asked him what he wanted to talk about and he just said, '*Come and meet me, we'll discuss it.*'

So the next Monday I met Charlie in town. He'd prepared a batch of forms he wanted me to fill in.

Until then, all the benefits for the two older kids, including Tammy's disability benefit, had been coming to me but Charlie now wanted me to sign them over to him since he was looking after them. And in order to do that, I had to put his name on their birth certificates.

I had no choice: the money was meant for the kids,

not me, and I couldn't take that away from them, even if Charlie was earning good money on the side.

He'd made an appointment at the Register Office for us to re-register the two births, and as we went in I could feel myself getting more and more upset.

Then, as I signed the certificates with Charlie's name now on them, I started crying. It felt like I was giving up my kids for good. What kind of a mother was I? I thought I had escaped him, but had I really? Would I ever be truly free?

The registrar was looking at me strangely. After all, it's not the kind of thing people cry about usually. But Charlie didn't say a word to her.

All he cared about was getting his money. When we'd finished he just walked out on his own and left me there with Thomas in the pram. I felt like I was letting my kids down so badly. They were mine yet it seemed like I'd just lost them for ever.

Without the extra benefits I was now forced to live on eighty pounds a week, which wasn't enough to pay for food and travel as well as the forty pounds per week which went towards the refuge.

Plus, Charlie now knew where I lived so there didn't seem much point me being in a safe house any more.

So Jennifer took me down to the council to put me on the list for a house, giving them the paperwork to show I was in a refuge, which would help me get priority.

It didn't take long at all. Within a couple of weeks I was allocated a two-bedroom house, not far from the kids.

Jennifer took me to look at it and it was quite nice, though only partly furnished.

'What do I do for furniture?' I asked Jennifer on the way back to the refuge. 'I don't own anything and I don't have any money.'

'Don't worry,' she said. 'There's an organisation run by the church. We'll give you a letter to take down there and you can get everything you need. But you have to get there early to make sure you get the best stuff.'

So the next morning, on a freezing cold day in March, I was stood outside the warehouse at 8 a.m., waiting for the doors to open at ten.

Stamping my feet and blowing on my hands, I waited for two hours with Thomas bundled up in his pram. By the time we got inside, we both had bright pink noses and numb fingers. But it was great there. They had loads of old furniture and white goods and I was taken round the warehouse to pick out all the stuff I needed.

I chose a cooker, washing machine, sofa, bedding, curtains, a microwave, vacuum and a table and chair set – all the furniture was free. The white goods only cost a fiver each, so in total I spent just twenty pounds to kit out my whole house. They stuck a label on my items and said they'd deliver it to the new place.

Okay, so it wasn't new but I didn't care. It was all good quality second-hand stuff and I couldn't afford to be choosy!

By the end of the week, Thomas and I were living in our own place and for the first time, I had to be entirely self-reliant. Strangely, the freedom that I wanted so badly was also frightening and hard. After so many years of being under Charlie's thumb, making decisions for myself was not at all easy.

And with only eighty pounds a week, I found it very difficult to make ends meet. Once I'd paid all my bills, I found I barely had enough money to buy food or nappies. I managed to get enough for Thomas but there was never enough left over to buy myself decent food.

Some weeks all I'd eat were cheap tins of tomatoes and toast. I got sick of it but I didn't have money for anything else. I could buy a dozen tins of tomatoes and three loaves of bread for under a fiver and that would have to do. The rest of the time I just drank water.

By now Charlie knew where I lived and we had an arrangement where I would have the two older kids over to my place every other weekend, then Charlie had Thomas on alternate weekends. So each of us either had all the kids or none at all. It was the weirdest situation. Here I was acting like a divorced wife with my own stepfather. But desperate to see the kids, I was forced go along with Charlie's latest twisted request.

Charlie could see I was struggling and tried to use it to his advantage – he'd invite me to go out for lunch with them if he had the kids on the weekend. And I'd say yes, just because I was starving.

'See what you're missing!' he'd tell me, as I wolfed down plates of chicken and chips. 'You can have all this if you come home.'

But I wasn't going to give in.

Then Charlie stopped paying for Thomas's nursery fees. It came as a complete surprise when I dropped him off one morning and the nursery administrator pulled me aside to tell me we were behind with our fees.

'What do you mean?' I said, bewildered. 'Charlie usually pays.'

'Well, he's missed the last four week's payment – you're now £400 in arrears.'

I didn't even realise Charlie had stopped paying, but now we owed hundreds of pounds!

That night I called him up.

'Can you please keep paying for Thomas's nursery?' I begged.

'Of course,' Charlie said. 'I'll pay them when you come home.'

Bastard! He was trying to make my life as hard as possible but it wasn't going to make me change my mind. Angry and humiliated, I had no alternative but to take Thomas out of nursery and create a payment plan to clear the unpaid fees.

The hardest thing was that when the kids came to me, I never had enough food to give them so Charlie brought round bags of chips and cartons of burgers, just so I had something to feed them. It was heart-breaking. I couldn't even put food on the table for my own children

Then Charlie started to use the kids against me. One Saturday morning he simply said he wasn't bringing the kids round and there was nothing I could do about it. I was totally at his mercy.

He also started seeing a woman called Cheryl and it wasn't long before Charlie was taunting me about this new relationship.

'She's great with the kids,' he'd tell me. 'She's going to be their new stepmum. We'll go away together and you'll never see them again.'

Now, whenever I picked up the children, Charlie refused to let me in the house so the kids had to come to the door while I stood in the street. He was making life harder and harder and I was getting more and more depressed.

By this time I'd made a friend across the road whose name was Gail. She'd lost a little boy so we had something in common and after a while we became good friends.

I used to pop over to her house, and, over time, I told her all about Charlie being abusive, going to live in the refuge and how he was using the kids against me.

It was the first time I had a proper friend without Charlie controlling anything about it and she'd invite me over for a drink and chat in the evenings.

But by August, I was really miserable and I'd started to drink just to try and block out the pain.

One sunny Saturday afternoon, when Charlie had the kids, I went over to Gail's place and we were outside her place on picnic chairs, drinking and chatting with her fella and Gail's brother.

At first it was really nice and we were having a good time, but the more I drank, the more depressed I became until, out of the blue, I found myself in floods of tears.

'Come on,' Gail said, looking concerned. 'I think it's time to get you home.'

She stood me up and walked me over the road to my house, where I fell through the front door. I got up on my hands and knees and crawled to the bottom of stairs, and up the stairs to bed. When I flopped down onto the bed, more tears escaped my puffy eyes. I couldn't stop bawling

Gail came and sat down next to me: 'What's wrong honey?'

I was so miserable and drunk by this time I didn't even think before I spoke.

'It's Charlie – he's my stepdad.'

Gail's eyes widened in shock. 'What the hell are you talking about?'

'He married my mum when I was a little girl, then he started abusing me and took me away and he made me live with him like we were a couple. And the kids… they're all his.'

Gail was distraught and horrified by my revelation. 'You've got to go and tell somebody,' she said. 'You've got to go to the police, Tina. It's not right.'

'No, I can't,' I whispered. 'I can't. He's got the kids and if I tell, I'll never see them again. He'll kill me.'

It was the first time I'd told anyone the truth but I trusted Gail. I knew she was on my side and I knew she wouldn't tell my terrible secret to anyone else. But she was insistent.

'If you go to the police, he'll never see the kids again,' she urged. 'They'll lock him up and you'll keep them for ever.'

But I knew it wasn't that simple. Even after all this time, I still felt that somehow I was to blame. It was one last shackle I'd never be able to break.

At the beginning of September I got an email from Charlie, every word of which made me feel sick to my stomach.

'*I love you,*' it read. '*Don't you love me? I miss you so much and want you back. We've had four kids together… How can you have kids with me and say you don't love me?*'

It went on and on and it made me feel disgusted with him, myself and the whole situation.

So I wrote him an email back. '*I don't love you – I never have. The only love I ever had for you was that of a dad – and you destroyed that. I want to be on my own now. I want to be free. I want to live my life and be normal without being controlled. I want to be able to see the kids without the fear of them being taken away. Why can't you let me be?*'

As soon as I pressed the send button, I started shaking with fear. What would he do now?

A week after that, Charlie raped me.

He was dropping the kids off for their weekend and I'd gone upstairs to get my diary from the bedroom when Charlie followed me up.

I jumped as I heard the door slam shut behind me.

'What do you want?' I said, shaking with fear. I could see he was all worked up.

'If I can't have you, I'll make sure no one else can,' he growled as he threw me down on the bed. Then he yanked my leggings and pants off me and raped me.

I wanted to scream for help but nobody would hear me but the kids and what could they do? How could they help?

Afterwards, he got up and started laughing. Then he walked out and went back downstairs.

I hated him more than ever at that moment but I also felt broken.

I took myself off to the bathroom and washed myself over and over again then I splashed water on my face, pulled my hair back into a ponytail and went back downstairs. Once again I felt like that helpless little girl. I didn't call the police, the same fear that was branded on to my soul stopped me. I'd reached a point where I couldn't even see the point of telling anybody.

Seeing the kids playing happily in the front room, I thought,'*I can't do this any more.*'

It was the last straw.

Chapter 19
Giving Up

'You're not getting the kids back,' Charlie's voice came slow and nasty on the phone. 'In fact, you're never seeing any of them again. I'm taking them away, somewhere you won't find us, and we're all going to start a new life together. This is the last you'll hear from me.'

Then he hung up. I'd been making my lunch in the kitchen but I just abandoned my half-made sandwich and walked like a zombie from room to room, wondering what to do next.

It was the weekend after the rape and, too terrified to argue, I'd allowed Charlie to come and pick Thomas up as usual in the morning. After all it was only ever me he hurt and he adored the kids – I thought it might help to appease him. But now, two hours later, he'd called to tell me his goodbyes.

I felt utterly defeated and worn down. The past few months had been getting harder and harder and now I knew it had been building up to this.

Charlie was never going to let me go – he was determined to break me and he knew the only way to do that was through the kids. I rang the police and they promised to send someone round, but no one came.

That was it – I'd hit rock bottom. I'd lost everything in the world that mattered to me and I just didn't care any more. If I didn't have my kids, I had nothing to live for.

So I sat at the laptop and wrote out my last will and testament. At the end, I wrote: '*Tell the kids I'm sorry and I love them.*'

Then I went out and bought a two-litre bottle of vodka from the convenience shop round the corner, came home and rooted around for all the pills I could find.

I had loads of old packets of antidepressants I'd never taken and some painkillers. Nothing mattered any more – if the kids were gone, I had nothing to live for.

Then I sat on the bed and started taking the pills, all washed down with vodka.

The scorching liquid burned my throat but I didn't care. I swallowed five pills at a time, all in the same mouthful and must have done that ten times.

There were no thoughts in my head of the consequences, I just knew it would end and I'd be with Tom again.

The police still weren't there and I didn't expect them to turn up.

So I called Charlie.

'You can keep the kids,' I slurred. 'I've had enough, you've won. You've got what you wanted.'

On my computer, one of Tricia's friends, White Angel, popped up on MSN and we started chatting but as the conversation went on I felt myself drifting and my mind becoming hazy.

The words seemed to swim in front of my eyes and obviously wasn't making much sense because after a while, White Angel typed: '*What's wrong?*'

I typed back: '*I've got a bottle of vodka and I've taken a load of pills.*'

The next thing I know my phone was ringing – it was her.

She was trying to talk to me, asking me what I'd done and where I was but I was now too spaced out to talk. So I hung up and walked out of the house, still carrying my phone. It rang again.

'Where are you?' she asked urgently.

'I'm out. I'm out and I'm walking.'

'Where are you going?' she demanded.

'I'm going to the grave. Because that's where I want to be when I die. I want to be with Tom.'

Nothing could stop me – I just wanted to lie down next to my boy and go to sleep so that I could be with him for ever.

The cemetery wasn't far from my house, I just had to turn right at the end of my road and then it was one long walk up the hill.

But as I got to the bottom of my road, I saw Charlie's black Mondeo pull up and he caught sight of me weaving uncertainly up the street and started laughing. He got out and shouted, 'You're being stupid now, aren't you?'

I could barely get the words out: 'No, you've won. You took the kids off me, you've got what you wanted.'

He laughed again and called me a whore then got back in the car and drove off.

I staggered on up the road, dragging my legs, which felt by now like they were made of concrete.

The phone went again. 'Hello?' I breathed.

'It's me,' said White Angel. 'Look, I've called for an ambulance. Hold on, Tina, don't give up. Someone's coming to get you.'

'I don't want no ambulance,' I said – then the world went dark…

I came to in a hospital bed but everything seemed blurry and I couldn't keep my eyes open. I drifted back to sleep again and must have been in and out of consciousness until the next day when all the drugs wore off and I woke up for real.

I squinted as the bright afternoon sunlight pierced my eyes.

'Are you okay, Tina?' a nurse was standing over me, looking at me intently.

'What happened?' I croaked.

'A woman in London called 999 and they sent an ambulance. They found you unconscious in the street, not far from your house. They pumped your stomach and you're now in A&E. We'll be transferring you to a ward soon; is there anybody you'd like us to contact to let them know you're here?'

And with that, I burst out crying, great heaving sobs. I just lay my head back on the pillow and let the tears flow.

'What's wrong?' she asked.

I just shook my head and spoke, my eyes fixed on the ceiling. 'I don't want to be here. I want to die. I just want to die.'

Later, they transferred me to the ward where the psychiatrist came to see me. I told him what had happened with the kids, told him about ringing the police and they hadn't come.

He just sat writing everything down and then asked me if I was still feeling suicidal. I told him I wasn't but inside, I still felt as bleak and hopeless as I had the day before.

He said he was going to discharge me and make an appointment for me to come and see him as an outpatient.

I didn't have any way of getting home so I rang my sister to ask her to pick me up.

'Why?' she quizzed. 'Where are you?'

'I'm in hospital.' I replied in a flat monotone.

'What are you doing there?'

'I overdosed.'

Lisa rushed out with Dave and they dropped me back home, where I insisted I wanted to be. I could barely look them in the eye and only gave them one-word answers to their questions and as soon as I was in the front door, I sent them away again.

I still didn't have any reason to live, and the first attempt hadn't worked, so I just wanted to try again.

Wearing the jeans and the T-shirt I'd had on since the day before, I walked into a freezing cold shower. Then I got out, still in my sodden clothes, and opened all the doors and windows in the house.

'*If the drugs won't kill me, I'll die from pneumonia*,' I reasoned.

Next, I found a pair of blunt scissors in the kitchen and sat down in the living room, trying to slit my wrists. My mind was a complete blank – I just wanted to go, be rid of this terrible life once and for all. But the scissors were too blunt and I had to go over and over the incisions just to draw blood.

I don't know how long I was doing this before two women came through the door, followed by a policewoman.

'What are you doing?' the first woman cried as she dived to grab the scissors out of my hand.

'What does it look like?' I shot back resentfully.

Then I started weeping. The two women explained they were from the mental health team and insisted on taking me back to hospital.

While we were waiting for the ambulance to arrive, the policewoman took me upstairs to change into some dry clothes.

I explained again how Charlie had taken the children and threatened never to bring them back and she said that because Thomas lived with me permanently, they could insist he return him. But I would have to fight for custody if I wanted the other two.

'You know, by doing this,' she nodded at the pathetic scratches on my arm. 'You're letting him win. And you're just making things harder for yourself.'

'What do you mean?' I said.

'If you want your kids, you have to fight for them. Don't give up. You think you're the only person who's been through this? You're not – and you're not alone. Let me tell you there are a lot of people that go through this but if you let it get to you, you won't have the strength to get up and fight again. And how would your kids feel if they didn't have a mum?'

By this time I was feeling so guilty at what I'd done, I started crying again.

'Your kids need you,' she said forcefully. 'They need their mum to be strong, to fight for them and to give them the love nobody else can give them. So don't give up Tina. Don't let him win!'

Her words had a powerful impact on me. For too long I'd kept Charlie's dirty little secret and it had nearly destroyed me. He'd controlled my life, kept me a virtual prisoner in his house and distanced me from the kids. If I died, he would warp their minds and their lives too and I couldn't let him do that. They deserved so much better.

There was something I had to do if we were ever going to be free.

Later that afternoon I was back in hospital, face to face with the same shrink I'd seen that morning.

But this time, I felt different.

'I want to go home,' I told him. 'I've got to get my little boy back.'

'Now if we let you out, you're not going to do something silly again, are you?'

'No,' I said adamantly. And I meant it.

I had other plans now.

Chapter 20
Reckoning

I walked into the support centre the next morning, shaking in anticipation of what I was about to do. For sixteen long years I'd kept Charlie's horrible secret, protecting him from the consequences of his crimes and put myself and my children in danger. But not any longer.

I found Jennifer in the office and she immediately saw from my expression that something was wrong.

'Can we talk?' I asked nervously.

She closed the door after me and I sat down.

'Charlie's not my partner, he's my stepdad,' I started. 'He's been abusing me since I was a little girl when he was married to my mum. We lived in another town back then but then they split up, I got pregnant by him at fourteen and he moved us here – it's gone on from there. We've had four kids together. He always said he'd kill me if I ever told anyone the truth but I need to tell someone now because he's threatened to take the kids away.'

Jennifer was clearly shocked but she let me talk until I told her everything. As the words came spilling out, I felt a great weight lifting off my shoulders.

'This is not your fault,' she said afterwards.

It was the first time anybody had said that to me and it came as a surprise – I expected, after staying with Charlie for sixteen years, that people would think I was to blame.

'Really, Tina,' she insisted. 'This isn't your fault. This hasn't been easy for you, coming here today but you've done the right thing.'

'What happens now?' I asked.

'Well, we've got to contact social services and let them know what you've told us. You must also go to the police and make a formal statement. We can put you in a safe house if you're afraid he'll come after you.'

'No,' I said. 'I've got to be further away. Actually, I've made plans to get out of the area. I can't be anywhere he can find me when the truth comes out. I'll let you know where I am when I arrive.'

I filled Jennifer in on the plans I'd made the night before, then once they had collected Thomas for me, we went home and waited for my brother Paul and his friend to come and get us. They were on their way up from Wales, where they'd agreed to let me stay with them. I'd already packed all our bags and kept them hidden in a cupboard upstairs in case Charlie turned up unexpectedly. I couldn't let him know what I was up to.

My mind racing, I wondered how long it would take social services to visit Charlie. And then what?

Would the kids be taken off him? I was in a new reality now – a reality where I didn't have to lie any more, where I could finally reveal who I was and what had happened to me for so long. It was scary. I just didn't know what was going to happen.

At midnight, Paul and his friend arrived and we packed all my stuff into the car, then I went to see Gail and told her that I was going.

'I have to do this,' I told her. 'Charlie's going to get what's coming to him but I can't be anywhere he can find me while this is happening.'

We held each other for ages and I let the tears roll down my face.

'You're a good friend,' I said. 'Thank you. I've never had a friend like you before.'

'You can count on me,' she said. 'Just look after yourself and keep your head up. I'm dead proud of you.'

Then we got into the car in the cold September night and slowly drove through the dark, deserted streets, Thomas asleep beside me on the back seat.

As we passed the cemetery, I made a silent promise to the little boy I was leaving there.

'I'll be back,' I said. 'I won't be away for ever. I'll come back for you one day.'

I didn't know how and I didn't know when but I knew I was coming back to see him.

The night wore on and I shed some tears as we put more and more distance between me and the town I'd lived in for most of my life, more distance between me and my two older children.

'*What now?*' I wondered.

Two days later I was at the reception desk in a Welsh police station, completely lost for words. The duty sergeant had only asked how he could help me and I was stumped. I didn't even know how to start!

Luckily, one of the women from the local Women's Aid centre had accompanied me there for moral support.

'We'd like to speak to someone please,' she said.

That helped and I suddenly found my voice. 'Yes, I'd like to speak to someone about reporting abuse,' I added.

'That's not a problem,' the policeman nodded. 'I'll just go and find a female officer and we'll take you through and interview you.'

It took five days in total to make my statement – every day for six hours straight I talked about everything that had happened to me since Charlie had come into my life. And though much of it made me cry, it felt so good to finally be letting it all out. I'd been silent too long.

It was scary but the police were very reassuring and told me over and over again that I was safe now.

And then they said again that it wasn't my fault. I knew what they meant, but it was going to take a long time for me to accept that.

The police officer looked at me intently as I shook my head and sighed. 'You're not to blame for this Tina,' she said again. 'He took advantage. He shouldn't have done it. It was him, not you. These are very serious crimes he committed.'

'*Him, not me. His fault, not mine.*' I had to keep telling myself that over and over again.

For so long I'd been petrified of telling anybody the truth about my life, afraid they would judge me, blame me for everything that had happened. After all, I had kids with Charlie.

But all these different people, these total strangers, kept telling me the same thing – it wasn't my fault.

Just as I'd anticipated, Charlie turned up at my empty house shortly afterwards to find me. Gail watched his car pull up outside my door and laughed as she saw him becoming more and more frustrated when I didn't answer.

Then she couldn't resist – she walked to her own front door and called out to him.

'She's not there, you know. She's gone. And you're not going to find her!'

She told me later on the phone his face was a picture and we both had a good laugh. I wish I'd been there to see it but at least I knew he couldn't get to me.

*

Within days, both social services and the police had been out to see Charlie. First social services put the kids on the child protection register – but for some reason that I didn't understand, they were still allowed to stay with their dad – and then the police pulled him in for questioning.

They kept me informed every step of the way.

'He's not denying the kids are his,' they told me the following week. 'But he says that you initiated a physical relationship when you were fifteen.'

Oh my God! My stomach turned over. I thought I was going to be sick right there. How could anyone think I wanted to sleep with my own stepdad?

'We're going to keep questioning him,' the policeman reassured me.

I put the phone down and sat in the living room in silence for an hour. Charlie knew how to lie and it seemed he'd dreamt up a plan of how to handle the police. He must have thought about this for years, I realised. He had been planning it all along – now what? Would the police believe me? Could he really manage to worm his way out of this? I'd seen him lie so many times, I knew how good he was at it. Now, it was him against me. Could I really win?

Four weeks after I left the Midlands, social services called to say they were going to see the children at school and asked if I wanted them to pass on any message. Just the mention of my kids made me ache inside.

'Tell them I love them, I miss them and I'll see them soon.'

A few hours later I got a call back. They said when they'd passed on the message, both Tammy and Alex had broken down in tears.

'He told them you were dead, Tina,' the social worker explained. 'He told them that you and Thomas had both died. So they were in shock when we told them your message.'

I was reeling. 'Bastard!' I breathed. 'How could he do that to them?'

'Don't worry,' the social worker reassured me. 'We told them the truth and we're keeping a close eye on them. They said they miss you too and want to see you soon.'

Tears soaked my cheeks. How long would I have to be away from them both? I had no idea.

In the midst of all this happening, I fell pregnant again. I'd just made a statement to the police which had taken days and everything was getting on top of me so Paul, and one of his friends and I got load of drinks in and got totally out of our heads. I was so drunk, I don't even remember having sex with him. I just remember waking up to find him sleeping beside me.

I didn't mean to sleep with him – it was a mistake, a one-night stand. I was that drunk I don't even remember what it felt like and I hadn't told either the father or social services that I was pregnant. What would they think? I was scared they'd think me irresponsible and not let me have the kids back. Plus, I didn't know what I was going to do about the baby – I didn't want another child, but at the same time, abortion was a scary thought.

A few days after I had talked to social services about my fears that Tammy and Alex were being neglected, I got a phone call from the police saying Charlie had been arrested and that they were going to be doing interviews. I was happy but at the same time I didn't know what to think – was he going to admit it? Blame me? All these things going over and over in my head. They interviewed him four times, and each time he kept changing his story. In one statement he said I was fifteen when he started having sex with me, but the police pointed out this couldn't have been true because I'd only just turned fifteen when I gave birth so I must have been at least fourteen when it began.

'He's tying himself in knots,' the police officer reported back. 'He can't actually stick to one story.'

'*Yes!*' I thought. '*All those bloody lies are catching up with him at last and he's making mistakes.*'

It felt like the tide was finally starting to turn against him. My statements had been utterly consistent throughout and it felt like everyone was on my side. It hit me then – they believe me. They all believe me.

*

A week later, I managed to find a way of contacting Alex. I knew he played an online game called Moonscape and one day I went into the game and created a profile for myself. Then I started searching for Alex in the game.

Eventually I found him – my heart nearly broke when he wrote: '*I miss you, Mum.*'

He gave me the house phone number and when Charlie was out, we managed to chat and catch up. I didn't know what to tell him about the case so I just reassured him over and over again that I was coming back soon and we'd be together again.

'How you getting on at home?' I asked.

'Mmm…all right, I suppose.' He didn't sound very convincing.

'How's Tammy?'

'Yeah, she's okay. She's right here, playing with her toys. She's a bit upset though.'

I closed my eyes and tried not to let the distress show in my voice. '*Where's your Dad now?*'

'He's at the pub.'

'Where's Daniel?'

'He's at his girlfriend's place.'

I realised then it was six in the evening and Alex and Tammy were alone in the house with no one to make them tea, bathe them or put them to bed. So I stayed on the phone, giving instructions to Alex to help him prepare some food for him and Tammy to eat that night. They seemed scared and lonely, but I tried to stay positive and upbeat.

'Just pour the beans in a bowl and put them in the microwave,' I directed. 'You can do that, Alex, because you've seen Mummy do it, haven't you?'

'*Yeah.*'

'Okay, well, you're just going to do what Mummy does.'

I stayed on the phone with him all that night until Charlie got back at ten – those poor kids were being completely neglected. But it didn't even occur to me at the time to ring the police. All I wanted was to make sure they could hear my voice and feel reassured.

The next day I rang social services and told them everything.

Charlie wasn't looking after these kids properly and I couldn't stand for it any longer – if they stayed with him, they'd be in danger.

'What can you do about it?' I asked them. 'My kids aren't getting fed, they're not getting looked after and I'm just sat here bloody worrying like crazy.'

They called me back ten minutes later. 'We've had a chat here,' my social worker Pippa said. 'And we've agreed they'd be better off with you. So, would you be willing to come back here if we got your kids back?'

I didn't hesitate. 'Of course!'

*

Two days later, and two months after I'd fled home, I found myself juddering up the M1 in a clapped-out old banger, praying it wouldn't break down. I'd eventually passed my test some years ago, but Charlie had rarely let me drive, so I was nervous.

I didn't want to ask Paul's friend for a lift again as he'd already gone out of his way to help me, giving us a roof over our heads when we needed it most.

So I'd gone out and found a second-hand car, which I paid just thirty-five pounds for, and in it I'd managed to squeeze in all the stuff we'd brought down eight weeks previously.

Poor Thomas was also squashed somewhere in the back, and for most of the journey, he was completely invisible under all our bags of clothes and toys. Still, we were going home and that was the important thing!

Social services had agreed to find me a one-bedroom flat, a safe house where Charlie couldn't find me, and I hoped to get up there by 6 p.m. to meet them and settle in to my new home.

But the car was useless and refused to get over sixty – it also kept threatening to overheat so I had to keep pulling it into every single service station on the motor-way to give it time to recover.

Eventually I crawled into town late that evening, exhausted and frazzled from our nerve-racking adven-ture and tried to contact social services, but they'd gone home for the night, obviously thinking I was going to come the next day.

I called my sister and she agreed to put me up at hers. Then I drove to my old house and knocked on Gail's door.

When she saw me, standing at the door with Thomas in my arms, she started screaming then wrapped her arms around me in the biggest hug imaginable.

'I thought I'd never see you again!' she grinned. 'I'm so glad you're back!'

We spent an hour catching up and I told Gail all about what had happened with the police and Charlie. Then I admitted I'd done something stupid.

'I had a few too many one night and I slept with a friend of Paul's,' I revealed. 'Now I'm pregnant.'

Gail let out a small giggle. 'You know what? I'm pregnant too!'

It was a bizarre coincidence and I could see how happy Gail was so I didn't tell her the truth about my own situation. I was torn – I still didn't know whether I was going to keep the baby.

As I left for my sister's, Gail gave me another big hug.

'You're doing so well,' she said. 'I know this isn't easy but keep your chin up. I'm here for you anytime.'

It felt good to be back home, back among friends and soon to be back with my family.

Chapter 21
Reunited

Early the next morning I rang social services and told them I'd arrived in the middle of the night and had to stay at my sister's.

'That wasn't very clever,' they said sternly. 'You're not safe there. Charlie could have found you.'

'I know. I need to get out of here.'

I realised while I was staying with Lisa that she'd been in regular contact with Charlie while I'd been in Wales. It seemed they'd got quite friendly and I was relieved I'd not told her that I was in Wales when I'd done a runner. She seemed pleased to have me back but the more time I spent with her, the more I realised that it was a little bit too close to home and I needed to distance myself from her and Charlie.

Later that day, I drove to the support centre and Jennifer met me there to show me to my new home. We pulled up to a large estate and my heart sank when I realised it was on the top floor of a large block of flats. We struggled up with the pram and some of the bags to a small, bare one-bedroom flat. The bedroom had a big double bed and a pair of bunkbeds. In the plain living room there was not much furniture: a settee, one armchair, a table and two chairs, and the kitchen and bathroom were both tiny.

I hunted about but couldn't find a washing machine, dryer, microwave or curtains. It was a good job I'd thought to buy a small telly.

'Right then,' I tried to put a brave face on it. 'I'd better get myself sorted out.'

Jennifer and I made several more trips to the car to unload the rest of the stuff. It was three weeks till Christmas and all I had to decorate the place was a mini fibre-optic Christmas tree and a few coloured paper rings Thomas had made.

I'd bought a couple of presents for Thomas while we were in Wales – a Thomas The Tank Engine floor mat with a pen you filled up with water and a wooden train set.

We put the tree on the table and the toys by the side of it. It looked very small and pathetic but I tried my best to look happy, for Thomas's sake.

'This is going to be our new home for a while,' I smiled. 'You've got a bunk bed – isn't that great? Now, why don't we go put your sheets on it?'

That evening I went round to Lisa's as she'd invited me and Thomas for tea, knowing I hadn't had time to do any shopping. We were all settled in front of the TV enjoying a tasty fish pie she'd bought from Asda when the phone rang.

'It's Charlie,' Lisa said, holding her hand over the receiver. 'He says he wants to talk to you.'

My stomach flipped over. I hadn't spoken to Charlie since the day he'd found me walking up to the graveyard to die and I really didn't want to speak to him now. After everything that had happened and me finally going to the police, I didn't want any contact with him at all.

I shook my head but Lisa insisted, 'Look, he says he just wants to talk to you about the kids. That's all.'

Reluctantly, I took the phone: 'Yeah, what is it?'

I was shaking.

'We need to talk about what we're going to do about the kids. Why don't you come to the house?'

'No, I'm not going to do that,' I said suspiciously.

'Well, why don't I come out to you?'

I certainly wasn't going to have him come to the safe house so I agreed that he could come to Lisa's place that night as long as she was there and would keep an eye on us.

Ten minutes later I heard his car pull up outside and he beeped his horn.

My sister stood at the door and I went to the car, steeling myself for what might happen.

Then I opened the car door and got in, making sure to keep the door open and my foot on the pavement, just in case he tried to grab me.

His face was set in anger. 'Why are you doing this to me?' he demanded. 'To the kids?'

'I'm not doing anything,' I said. 'I've done nothing wrong.'

'Yes you have!' he shot back. 'You're dragging me and the kids through a pile of shit and it's all your fault. You don't have to make all our lives a nightmare.'

'It's not my fault what's happened,' I retorted, suddenly remembering all the things people had been telling me the past two months. '*You* did this to me. I just want my life back. I just want to be happy and for you to leave me alone.'

'Well, you're making the kids miserable.'

'You were the one who told them I was dead!'

I'd been away from Charlie for eight weeks and in that time I'd grown a lot stronger. I was still scared of him – I still am to this day – but I wasn't scared to speak my mind any more.

After a short silence, he asked, 'So, do you want the kids for the weekend?'

I think he was tired of not getting time off to indulge himself with his new girlfriend, or maybe he thought that if he was cooperative, I'd drop the charges. Either way, I didn't care – all I wanted was to see my children again.

He said he'd let me take them on one condition – that he could take Thomas back with him in the car to see Daniel, who missed him.

It was a big risk but I knew it was true about Daniel. Daniel and Thomas had a special bond; he would have been missing him like mad. Plus, Charlie knew that if he tried to keep Thomas, the police would only make him bring him back. So I agreed to let him take Thomas for an hour, after which he said he'd bring all the kids back to me.

I watched the minutes tick slowly by as I sat on the settee by the window, willing Charlie's car to return.

I leapt up as soon as I saw the Mondeo turn into the road and ran to the door to greet Alex and Tammy as they jumped into my arms, crying.

We went into the living room and Tammy wouldn't let me go! She sat on my knee and just kept her arms locked around my neck while Alex cuddled my knees.

It was so wonderful to see them after so long and I wept with happiness.

Thomas was back too and Daniel slipped in behind the others, with a slim blonde girl by his side.

'Who's that?' the girl asked him as she witnessed our emotional reunion.

'That's my mum,' he replied.

It suddenly hit me that although the truth had been told to the authorities, the one person who still didn't know the whole story was Daniel. '*Poor kid,*' I thought. '*At some point, someone's going to have to tell him that I'm not his mum, I'm his sister.*'

'Right then,' Charlie said. 'I've brought all their stuff – when do you want me to pick them up?'

'I'll drop them back at Lisa's on Sunday and you can come for them here,' I said carefully. There was no way I was going to let him know the address of the safe house!

An hour later we were all back in my small, one-bedroom flat – Thomas, Alex, Tammy and me. The kids ran around the place, excited and curious to be in a new house.

'Bunkbeds!' Alex shouted jubilantly. 'Brilliant!'

I was so happy – we were all together at last and we had a whole weekend to enjoy being a family. The next day I took the kids out shopping for food and we went to play in the park. Alex and Tammy filled me in on the past two months. Daniel was seeing a new girl, Steph, – the one who came to the house – they'd only been going out two weeks but both kids seemed to like her.

Later that night I tucked them all up – the boys had the bunkbeds while Tammy shared the double bed with me. Watching them all sleeping soundly, I realised something. There was no way I could let them go back to Charlie. '*I can't do it,*' I said to myself over and over. '*I can't send them back.*'

It seemed with each passing day, my frazzled mind slowly became a little clearer. I had to protect these children.

So the next morning I rang the police and explained everything – about the case, Charlie's behaviour and about taking the kids for the weekend.

'The thing is, social services don't know the children are with me,' I said. 'I'm in a safe house and I don't want to send them back to their dad. Can I keep the kids? Would I get into trouble if I did that?'

'Miss, they're your kids,' the officer said. 'By law you can keep them if you want to. But I suggest you ring social services first thing Monday morning and explain what's happened.'

I thought long and hard about all the possible consequences and eventually, I made up my mind.

I rang Lisa to tell her what I'd decided. It didn't take long for word to get back to Charlie.

When he called I tried to stay calm.

'What do you mean you're keeping them?' he yelled.

'They're staying with me now,' I said. 'I've spoken to the police and they said I'm within my rights. I don't think it's a safe place for them right now.'

He went mad but I just put the phone down. Later he sent through a series of text messages. '*I've spoken to the police and I know where you are now,*' he wrote. '*I'm coming down to get the kids.*'

I panicked – how could he know where I lived? What had the police told him? I couldn't believe they would give away the address of a safe house so I called the station again and asked if Charlie had rung and if he knew where I was living.

'There's no record of that call,' said the duty sergeant. 'And I can assure you – we wouldn't divulge the whereabouts of a safe house. I think he's having you on.'

I put the phone down and smiled to myself. *'He's lying,'* I thought. And his scare tactics weren't going to work on me any more. I was beyond that.

I made sure I had enough medication for Tammy for the next day, and then put the kids to bed that night and told them that they weren't going back to their dad.

'So you're staying here with me now,' I finished.

'And you're not going to go away again, Mummy?' Tammy asked as I tucked her little bear in next to her.

'No, I'm staying here with you. And we're going to be together. For ever.'

Chapter 22
Revelation

Now I was on my own with the three kids in a one-bedroom flat. Though it was great to be together again, I have to confess that in that first year I struggled.

It wasn't just the fact that I now had two legal cases going on – the criminal case against Charlie and the case in the family courts to decide where the kids would live permanently. I was pregnant, on my own, with no money and had spent so long under Charlie's thumb, I struggled to connect to the children.

Just sitting next to Alex sometimes made me feel uncomfortable – if he plonked himself down on the sofa next to me, I could feel my heart starting to race and my breath getting shorter. I suppose it was like a panic attack and I'd only feel better again when he moved away. I got help from the regeneration team, who were like a family support unit. They sent out a key worker twice a week to help me get closer to the kids.

When I opened the door to the support worker from the regeneration team, I was surprised to see it was

Angela, one of the women from the mother-and-baby unit all those years ago.

My heart thudded – what would she think of me? I felt ashamed that she now knew everything about Charlie but she just smiled and gave me a big hug.

'It's good to see you again, Tina' she said. 'It's been a long time.'

In that first session I told her everything that had happened and she just sat there, shaking her head.

'I'm really sorry,' she said when I'd finished. 'I wish I could have done something all those years ago. I didn't have a clue.'

'It's okay,' I said. 'It's not your fault. It's just one of those things.'

Afterwards, she got me and the kids round the floor in the living room and we played Pick-Up sticks and Kerplunk. It was great – Charlie had never let us have games in the house and it was fun to be doing something all together.

Afterwards she explained, 'We need to help you bond with the kids. It's really good you're being honest about your feelings. But the more stuff you can do together as a family, the better you'll be able to communicate with them.'

I came to really look forward to Angela's appointments every week. For one thing, it was nice to work with someone I knew and also I felt that all the activities we did together brought my family a little bit closer. And through these visits I also decided that I would keep my unborn child – I hoped that a new baby would help bond my little family closer together.

She'd unroll her plastic mat on the floor and we'd play games, make stuff or cook. One time we all made little paper plate men with pipe cleaner legs and arms.

Another time she taught us how to make hedgehog muffins. The kids loved it too, and slowly I began to feel the barriers coming down.

Angela's visits were certainly a relief from the constant meetings and appointments for the cases, which were horrible.

Charlie had now been charged but he was out on bail, and this meant the kids still had to be on the At Risk Register. There were bail conditions too: he couldn't speak to us or come within 500 metres of us.

But he was there at those meetings, and it was sickening every time I saw him.

At the first meeting of our family case, I was shocked to see how many people were now involved. Seated round the table were my solicitor, Charlie, his solicitor, the police, two representatives from social services, a reviewing officer and his assistant, the health visitor and Jennifer from the support centre.

Eleven of us in total! Even though most of those people were on my side, I felt guilty and uncomfortable, like I'd caused a lot of trouble.

The reviewing officer outlined everything that had happened until that point and I looked over at Charlie to see him leaning back casually in his chair, as if he didn't have a care in the world.

My heart leapt when she said Charlie would never get the kids back again but she concluded by saying that they had to make a decision about whether I was capable of looking after them on my own. My children would either stay with me or go into care.

I wasn't going to let that happen – I hadn't come this far to give them up now.

But Charlie had other ideas. 'She can't look after them properly,' he said. 'She's no good with Tammy and her health problems.'

'That's a lie!' I erupted.

'Shhh! Please be quiet,' my solicitor tried to calm me down. 'It's all getting noted.'

But how could I ignore it? I was the one who took Tammy to hospital whenever she was ill, I gave her her injections and administered her medicines.

Now I knew what Charlie was up to. He thought he'd bad mouth me to ensure I didn't keep the kids. That's how selfish he was! If he couldn't have them, he wasn't going to let me keep them. He'd rather they went into care than live with their own mother!

But I wasn't going to let him get away with it.

So I turned to my solicitor: 'It's true, Tammy's got ongoing health problems. But she's now eight years old and she can do a lot of the things she needs herself.'

My blood was boiling and I wanted to scream and shout. The whole reason I'd finally turned Charlie in to the police was to protect the children.

Meanwhile I struggled on at home. By now Thomas was two-and-a-half and a real handful. He'd abandoned his normal bedtime so every time I tried to put him down at 7 p.m., he'd be up again, running around the living room, so I'd try and put him down again. This would go on and on for hours until, finally exhausted, he'd fall asleep at 1 a.m. Then on the dot of five he'd be up again!

Exhausted, I'd have to get the other kids up and get them to school, all the way across town.

It would take forty minutes to walk into town then we'd have to get a bus to take them up to their schools. After I'd dropped them off, I'd have to come all the way back again with Thomas.

We were living out of bin bags because we had no washing machine and had to take all the clothes to the launderette, and on top of all that I had constant appointments about Tammy's condition and meetings for the cases.

At one point the police came out to take a DNA swab from Alex.

'In case Charlie ever denies being the father,' they explained.

*

'I'm sorry kids,' I apologised as I put Christmas dinner on the table. 'It's not the full works but we'll just have to make the most of it.'

That year we had turkey roll and chips with beans for our Christmas lunch – it was all I could afford.

I could have cried. Charlie was still getting all the benefits for the kids so I had no money to buy a proper Christmas dinner or even any presents.

I was told that after twelve weeks the benefits would automatically start coming to me, but in the meantime we were living off eighty pounds a week. After the gas, electricity, launderette and all the buses to and from school, I had literally nothing left.

Every week I had to ask social services for food vouchers just so I could do a full week's shopping.

Fortunately, the support centre were very supportive. They donated a few toys for the older kids, and the week before Christmas they invited us all to their annual party.

They'd decorated the place with loads of tinsel and streamers and all the other mums and their kids were there so the kids had loads of fun dancing and racing about.

They also put on a lovely spread and we pigged out on meat and potato pie, mushy peas, beetroot and butter pie. The butter pie was just potatoes and onions but it was gorgeous and I went up for a second helping, after all, I was eating for two now!

There were chocolate selection boxes for every child and afterwards, one of the staff dressed up as Santa Claus and handed out gifts.

As we left Alex asked if we could take home one of the plastic Father Christmas decorations to hang up in our flat.

When we got back, we hung it over the fibre-optic tree and put all the selection boxes next to it so they had something to enjoy on Christmas day.

Two days later, the support centre came round with a big hamper filled with fruit and veg, Christmas pudding, biscuits, cakes, tins of beans, and tea and coffee.

Tears stung my eyes as I emptied out the box – it meant a lot to me that these kind people were helping us but at the same time I felt so guilty I couldn't give my children anything for Christmas and we were relying on handouts. Even their clothes had been donated by the support centre.

'I can't thank you enough,' I told Jennifer later that day on the phone.

'Don't mention it,' she said. 'Just remember, it isn't always going to be like this. You'll be up on your feet soon enough.'

January came around and the freezing cold and long trips to school and the launderette were beginning to drain my energy reserves.

On top of that, I was now attending parenting

courses, going for psychological assessments and had what felt like a constant stream of meetings, appointments and check-ups – and there were also visits to the doctor to make sure that everything was progressing smoothly in my pregnancy.

It was all beginning to drag me down.

Then, one morning in February, Karen, the police officer who'd been dealing with my case from the beginning, called with some news.

'We've found another victim,' she said. 'Tina, it wasn't just you. He'd done it before.'

At that moment I felt a lurch in my stomach and ran to the toilet to throw up.

After all these years of believing he'd singled me out, it was a dreadful shock to find out that it wasn't just me.

'Why didn't they go to the police before?' I asked Karen.

'Probably for the same reason as you,' she said. 'She was scared. Also, it happened quite a few years ago. I guess she thought she'd try and put it behind her and move on.'

They'd uncovered the second victim while making their normal enquiries about the case and this woman said she would be willing to go to court to testify against Charlie.

I was elated – with another victim, our case was now much stronger.

Up till that point, I'd not felt very confident that Charlie would be found guilty. Even though it was proven that Alex was his son, he was insisting I was a willing participant in the relationship and because of how much he'd managed to fool people in the past, I thought he'd wriggle his way out of this too.

But now there was another victim like me, it wasn't going to be so easy for him to explain us both away. The news couldn't have come at a better time – it was just the lift I needed to get through the next few months.

'*You can do this*,' I told myself. '*Don't give up!*'

From that point on, things started looking up. Social services found us a nice three-bedroom house, near the kids' schools. With the extra space, they had more room to play and there were plenty of other kids around for them to get to know.

They were now taken off the At Risk Register and put on care orders, which meant that social services had shared parental responsibility with me.

The only thing was, we were now round the corner from Charlie, and though our day-to-day lives were easier, I felt a constant unease because I knew I could bump into him at any time.

'He's on bail conditions which prevent him coming near you or the kids,' my social worker reassured me. 'Even if you see him, he can't do anything.'

But it wasn't that straightforward – I did catch sight

of Charlie now and again, and every time I felt ill. Having him practically on my doorstep just made me worry all the time.

I saw him a few times when he came to the corner shop near my house – I'd always dive back inside the moment I set eyes on him.

By now Charlie was only allowed to have contact with the children during supervised visits at the children's centre, not far from our new home.

I'd drop them off for an hour and one of the workers had to stay in the room the whole time he was there.

But, eventually, Charlie's visits were stopped altogether because he refused to stick to the rules and broke his bail conditions time and time again.

The teachers at Alex and Tammy's schools had seen him hanging around the playground, trying to catch sight of the kids, and had called social services. It was such a relief once the visits ended.

Tammy had been assessed in the hospital and they decided that although she was doing fine, she was an ideal candidate for a bone marrow transplant. It would give her a whole new immune system and clear up many of her problems; in addition, social services believed that Tammy would benefit from the transplant.

The doctors had tested blood taken from Thomas's umbilical cord when he was born and discovered that he was a perfect match for her. But just going along to the doctors meetings in the outpatient ward of the children's hospital was hard for me – it was where my son had died just three years before. And back then they'd wanted to do a transplant on Tom so I already knew what was involved; I knew she'd have to go through chemotherapy to kill off her immune system beforehand.

The doctors tried to reassure me.

'Thomas is a perfect match,' they said. 'And he's a sibling donor which means that her body has a much higher chance of accepting the bone marrow.'

'But what about the risks of infection?' I asked. 'I've seen this before – I've been through it – and I don't want to go through it again!'

As we walked to the car park after the meeting, I told Pippa I didn't think I could face watching Tammy go through a transplant. I just couldn't cope with any more worry or the prospect of losing another child. I was so weary.

'Look, you want the best for her, don't you?' she said.

'Of course I do,' I shot back. 'But have you ever lost a child? Do you know what that's like? Every time I come back to this place, I relive it over and over again. When I walk through those corridors I see myself carrying Tom in my arms up and down, trying to comfort him. I replay in my mind all those times I sat in that cafeteria spoonfeeding him, willing him to eat and be strong. I can't go in there without all that coming back to me.

'And then…' I broke down in tears. 'And then he died in there. Do you know how difficult it is for me to even set foot in that place? What if I lost her too?'

'It's not going to be the same,' Pippa said gently. 'Tom is gone and now you have to concentrate on your kids who are here. It's the right thing to do, for her sake.'

My head sank to my chest – I knew I couldn't win this battle. I knew I had to put Tammy's needs first. Maybe I was being selfish but on top of everything else – my pregnancy and dealing with the man who abused me and kept me captive for sixteen years – dealing with my daughter's illness and the possibility, however remote, was just too much of a strain.

'I can't lose another one,' I said quietly. 'It would kill me.'

Chapter 23
Return

Despite my misgivings and with the assurances of the doctors involved that they would do everything they could to keep Tammy safe, I agreed to go ahead with the bone marrow transplant and the date was set for just two months before I was due to give birth.

But in the weeks before the transplant, I barely slept, tormented by all the possible outcomes.

It felt like déjà vu – here I was, heavily pregnant, taking another child to hospital for a bone marrow transplant.

They'd already prepared Thomas for what was going to happen.

'We have to let him know that he's going to be the donor,' the doctor explained.

'I know but he doesn't understand,' I protested. 'He's three and a half – how can he understand what bone marrow even is, let alone agree to let you take it!'

They talked me through everything that would happen and it was decided Thomas and Alex would go into foster care while I was in hospital with Tammy.

*

The foster carer was a lovely lady but it broke my heart that day when I had to leave my boys there. We'd packed all their clothes and toys up in big plastic sacks and we drove to the house, not knowing when I'd be able to have them back again.

Alex and Thomas were both crying when it was time for me to go.

'I love you both very much,' I told them. 'But this is something Mummy has to do to help your sister get better. Now, you be good boys and I'll see you both very soon.'

The next day, Tammy and I walked back into the hospital – the place that would be our home for the next two months.

The room they'd set aside for us was lovely. It had two beds, an ensuite bathroom, a telly and even a PlayStation.

Tammy hung her favourite drawings round the room and dotted her toys about so it would feel more like home. then we sat down and chose our dinner for that night from the menu.

'How you feeling?' I asked Tammy that night as we cuddled up on the bed watching *X Factor*.

'Mmm, a little scared,' she said. 'But I'm glad you're here.'

I was scared too, petrified actually, but I tried to smile to put Tammy's mind at rest.

Later that night, after she'd fallen asleep, I went

to sit in the car, and there I put my head on my arms and wept.

'Blood test time!' the nurse sung as she came into our room the next morning. 'Now, all little girls who give blood get a special prize in this hospital!'

They were trying their best to make this easier on her and after they'd taken blood, they rewarded her with a Little Mermaid bedding set.

We immediately put it on her bed and it gave the room a lovely personal feel.

Over the next few days, as Tammy had test after test to prepare for the chemotherapy, the friendly nurses showered her with toys and gifts. She got pens, pencil cases and a big musical waterfall toy, all brand new!

One night we played *X Factor* with them, borrowing the karaoke machine from the hospital's toy cupboard. All the nurses came in, one by one, and auditioned for us and we marked them out of ten.

It was really fun for Tammy and kept her mind off the treatment to come.

Eventually, they started her on the chemo, which they gave her through a drip in her arm. I was terrified of infection but the nurses were very careful and we were in our own room so it didn't feel unsafe.

Tammy was now getting very tired and she couldn't keep her food down. She had to be on a special 'clean diet', which meant that anything we opened had to be eaten or thrown away after twenty-four hours. But she stopped being able to taste anything because the treatment wiped out her taste buds and in the end the only thing she wanted to eat was curry!

One morning, seven days after the chemo started, she sat up in bed and a whole mass of hair stayed on her pillow.

As soon as I saw that, I started to cry. Tammy had beautiful long brown hair that hung down her back almost to her hips, but the chemo was making it fall out. She was very weak by now, so I sat her on the chair, and started to brush it. But every time I put the brush through it, clumps of hair came out.

'I don't think I'm doing much good here,' I said, as I pulled another handful of hair from Tammy's head. 'We knew this would happen, love. It's up to you. Do you want me to keep brushing?'

'No, just cut it off,' she said. 'I'll be okay, Mum.'

I was so proud of her at that moment – it was such a brave decision to make for one so young.

So we called in the specialist nurse and explained that Tammy wanted her hair cut off and we made it into a fun game.

The nurse brought in some clippers, scissors and a mat and I invited Tammy to step into my 'salon', pretending I'd just opened a hairdresser's.

'Now, what can I do for madam today?' I put on my best hairdresser's voice.

'I want something really different,' Tammy said, getting into the spirit of it. 'Just get rid of it!'

With every snip of the scissors, I felt terrible. I couldn't believe I was doing this to my own daughter. In the end we got the clippers and shaved off all her hair. And that was it; it was gone. The hospital had already ordered a wig to be made for her and she'd chosen one with long, black plaits stuck onto a bandanna. So it looked like a hat with plaits coming down.

But she never wore it. She was never ashamed of how she looked and was happy to walk around showing off her newly shaved head. She was so brave. I'd wince when I thought of what I'd been like at her age. It was the last time I'd been truly happy, before Charlie had destroyed my life. And now here was Tammy, clinging on to hers.

Three days later Tammy had her final round of chemo and for me that was a great relief. With Tom, we'd never got to that stage so getting Tammy through the chemo part was really important. Next, I had to go and pick up Thomas to bring him back to the ward, so they could take his bone marrow.

He was only due to be in for the one night and they'd put him in a different room on the same ward as Tammy. That night, I was torn between the two of them. My sick daughter or my young son who'd not seen me for two weeks? It was an impossible choice.

The following morning I went down to theatre with him and held his hand as they put him under. Then they stuck a long needle in his hip and harvested the marrow.

The doctors warned that his hip might be sore for a few days, but hours later, after he'd come round, I was delighted to see him running up and down the hospital ward.

The next day Tammy was due to have the bone marrow put in. She was connected up to a drip and the marrow, a funny yellowish colour, was then fed into her through the Hickman line she'd had inserted earlier in the week.

It was a nerve-racking process and the doctor had to stay in the room for the whole hour it took for the drip to feed into her.

Every ten minutes, he'd check her temperature and blood pressure. I was a bundle of nerves the whole time, hoping and praying the marrow would be accepted. If her body rejected it, the staff were on standby with drugs to counteract the rejection.

When he'd finished, the doctor told me that Tammy was stable and the transplant had gone as well as could be expected.

From this moment we were in permanent isolation to minimise the risk of infection. Tammy wasn't allowed out of the room at all until the bone marrow began to take effect. And only me, the nursing staff and our social worker Pippa were allowed inside the room with her.

The days passed by slowly. Tammy was now very weak and could only manage a few minutes of reading or watching TV before she had to have a sleep. And I kept vigil by her bedside. My only relief from the constant fear and worry were my nightly visits to the car, where I'd sit and cry, just to let out all my anxiety.

Three days after the transplant my social worker Pippa took me aside and asked if Charlie could visit Tammy at the hospital.

He had been kept informed about the transplant through social services and even though the supervised visits had been stopped, he was demanding to see her in hospital. What could I do? I couldn't say no because Tammy still loved her dad and really wanted to see him too.

'Okay,' I agreed. 'But what do I do when he's here? I don't want to see him.'

Pippa arranged for me to wait in the parents' room across the hall when he visited.

Tammy was still very ill at this point – it was just days since she'd had her transplant and she wasn't her normal, perky little self. She was tired and withdrawn but when we said her dad was coming to see her, she was thrilled. It made me happy just to see her smile again, even if it was because of Charlie.

So I went into the town centre the next morning and bought her a new pink tracksuit so she could look nice for her dad when he came later that day. We helped her put it on and then we all waited for Charlie to arrive.

We waited, and waited, and waited. Finally, after two hours Pippa rang Charlie on his mobile to find out why he was delayed.

I nearly screamed in frustration when she told me what he'd said – apparently he'd got lost on the way to the hospital and in the end he decided to turn around and go home.

'How could he get lost?' I whispered to Pippa, trying not to let Tammy know what I was saying. 'Do you know how many times he came here when Tom was ill?'

I couldn't believe it. Poor Tammy was so looking forward to seeing him and now it was me who had to break the news. She broke down into tears as soon as I told her. I was furious with Charlie but also so sad for Tammy. How could he do this to her?

'He'll come another day,' I promised as I held my crying girl.

So it was rearranged for two days later and, just like the last time, we dressed Tammy in her new pink tracksuit.

She was so excited, she told me all the things she wanted to show her daddy, like her Hickman line, her new toys and of course her bald head!

Then, at about 2 p.m., Pippa got a call on her mobile. 'He's in the car park,' she said, turning to me.

My hands started to shake and my heart was pounding – just knowing that he was near made me nervous. The nurse then took me to the parents' room and Pippa stayed in the room with Tammy.

As soon as I heard footsteps, I closed the door and pulled the blind over the window. Then I sat down and waited. Then, after a few minutes, I heard Charlie shouting. *'What the hell's going on?'*

I opened the door a crack to get a look at what was happening and my mouth fell open in horror.

Charlie was trying to force his way into Tammy's room and all the nurses were pushing him back, to stop him getting in.

'You knew you couldn't go in,' Pippa was shouting. 'She's in isolation. You knew about this, Charlie. You can speak to her through the glass but you can *not* go into the room with her. It's for her safety! Now calm down!'

'She's my daughter!' Charlie yelled. 'You can't stop me going in.'

Meanwhile, poor Tammy looked like she was in shock – she was holding her teddy close to her and weeping as Charlie continued to shout and swear.

Finally, one of the nurses alerted security and they took control of the situation, grabbing Charlie by an arm each and marching him out of the building.

He'd barely been there five minutes and in that whole time, he hadn't said one word to Tammy, the daughter he'd insisted so vehemently on seeing – the little girl who'd endured chemotherapy and a bone marrow transplant just days before.

She'd been so excited her dad was coming and now she was in floods of tears and really upset.

'He's not seeing these kids any more,' I said to Pippa. 'Never again. He doesn't give a toss about them. It's over. He can't do this.'

And she agreed. From that point onwards, all visits were stopped and he was only allowed to write to them – monitored, of course, by social services.

At the end of June, Tammy was well enough to come home and the next month I was due to be induced.

Social services were sceptical about whether I could cope with a baby, especially given all of Tammy's complex needs. But I assured them that mothering was all I'd known since I was barely a teenager myself.

'Looking after kids comes naturally to me,' I said. 'I know what they need and I know how to make a household work.'

Even so, at one meeting, they handed me a sheet with a routine organising my chores during the day. It was laid out hour by hour, starting at six in the morning and finishing at eleven at night. It felt ridiculous. Their control was so overwhelming at times, it felt like I'd just swapped one domineering parent for another!

I was so relieved when, after a week of being back home, Tammy was well enough go out into the garden without any problem. We were now in semi-isolation, which meant that we still couldn't have the boys back for fear of them bringing in an infection. We couldn't go into town or mix with other kids so we had to do all the shopping online and were more or less living like prisoners in our little house.

I was due to be induced a week later and so Tammy had to go to a foster carer while I was in hospital, but she went to a different foster carer to the boys because of the risk of infection.

My family were all over the place and I just hoped and prayed this labour would be quick so we could be back together again soon. In the end, it took them seven days to get the baby out of me! But at least that was seven days when my mind was taken off Charlie and the impending court case.

Matthew's birth was worse than all the others put together. They induced me every day for a week and eventually, I went into labour.

At 6 p.m. I was four centimetres dilated so they sent me up to the delivery suite, where they gave me gas and air. But I was in so much pain, I felt like I was dying.

'Please,' I begged the midwife when I finally saw someone coming to my room. 'Please, I need some pain relief. I'm in trouble here!'

But they were very short-staffed that day and the midwife said she'd try and get something sorted out for me as soon as she could, but she was extremely busy.

I just couldn't get comfortable and the only way I got any sort of relief was by lying on my side and curling up into a ball. But every time I did that the baby monitor round my belly lost connection with the baby's heartbeat and all the midwives would rush to my bed, thinking the baby was in distress.

'It's the only way I can bear it!' I screamed.

'Okay,' my specialist midwife said. 'In that case, we'll put a monitor clip on the baby's head.'

So I lay on my back while they attached the clip to the baby's head, which would keep monitoring the heartbeat until he was born.

By then I was delirious with pain so when I heard the two monitors beeping away, I panicked.

'No, No, NO!' I screamed. 'Put one back!'

'Put what back?' the midwife asked.

'Put that baby back! I'm not having twins. I don't want twins!'

She started giggling then – I was so out of it, I'd mistakenly thought the second monitor meant another heartbeat and therefore another baby.

'It's okay,' she said. 'Try and stay calm. You're not having twins. It's just the second monitor.'

So I lay back down again and twenty minutes later I got the urge to push.

'I'm pushing,' I said, after buzzing another midwife.

'No, don't be silly,' she replied. 'You can't be pushing. We only measured you twenty minutes ago and you were four centimetres dilated. If you push now the baby will get stuck and you'll end up having an emergency Caesarean.'

'I'm telling you,' I screamed. 'This baby's coming! I can feel it and I want to push this baby out.'

I begged them over and over again to examine me and finally one midwife gave in. She nearly had kittens when she saw the baby's head halfway out. Then it was a quick dash before he came flying out of me!

For seven days Matthew had resisted leaving my womb, but when he finally agreed to join me in the world, he didn't waste his time. The whole labour had been two hours from start to finish.

'What an awkward little boy you've been,' I scolded gently as I held him in my arms for the first time. He was eight pounds three ounces and gorgeously chubby.

*

I stayed in hospital for two days; then as soon as they let me out, I went straight round to see the boys with their new baby brother. After they'd cooed over him a little while, I took them to see the new Harry Potter film.

By September Tammy's blood tests results were back and they showed the transplant was a success and now Tammy had a proper immune system. She now had the same blood in her as Thomas. I tried not to think about how half that blood was Charlie's too and instead focused on watching my little girl get stronger by the day. Her hair was even starting to grow back.

By October, we were all reunited once more, and in early December the family case was concluded. It was decided that I would be allowed to keep the children: I had proved myself to be a good mum, and social services were satisfied that I could cope with having all the children on my own.

Finally, things seemed to be going well for me, and with my lovely children all together I was planning the best Christmas ever!

Chapter 24
Justice

For the first time since I was a child, Christmas that year was fantastic.

In the weeks beforehand, I'd bought loads of toys for the kids, a big plastic tree from Argos and tonnes of sparkly decorations which we hung all around the house.

I cooked a massive Christmas dinner with real roast turkey, spuds, carrots, Yorkshire puddings – the lot!

And as I looked round the table at my hearty brood tucking into their overflowing plates, I felt a geniune sense of happiness flooding through me.

By now the criminal case against Charlie was fast approaching and in February I got a call from Karen Howarth to say the date had been set for Spring 2008.

To prepare me for the trial, they took me to look around the courtroom where I'd be giving evidence.

'Oh my God!' I breathed as I swung open the big double doors. 'It's massive.'

'That's why we wanted you to see it,' said Kim, the representative from Witness Care. 'We don't want you to feel intimated on the day.'

She explained where everybody would sit – the benches for the prosecution and defence lawyers, the judge's bench and then she pointed to a box higher up than everything else. 'That's the witness stand. Go on,' she urged. 'Get up there and see how you feel.'

So I climbed into the box and surveyed the massive courtroom. Even in that empty room with just three people in it, I felt scared and intimidated.

'The two rows of benches facing you are the where the jury sit,' she carried on. 'Charlie will sit over there and the two benches next to you are the public gallery.'

'What does that mean?' I asked.

'The public are allowed to come in and sit in on trials,' she said. 'It's because we have an open justice system.'

'*How odd,*' I thought. '*Who on earth would want to come in and listen to the horrors of what someone like Charlie had done?*' I stood there for a while, trying to imagine what it would feel like to face Charlie in court and my heart started racing.

'You can have a screen up if you like,' Kim offered. 'If you give your evidence behind a screen, you don't have to face him. We'll bring you in and out of court through the judge's entrance.'

I knew this day would finally come when I'd have to give evidence against him but until this moment, I didn't know how I'd feel. Now I knew: I'd be terrified.

'I don't think I can face him,' I said. 'I'll do it behind the screen.'

Every time I had seen him – going to the corner shop or just in the street – he had scared the hell out of me. Giving evidence against him was just going to be much harder if I had to do it with him looking at me.

As the day of the hearing approached, I steeled myself for the courtroom ordeal ahead. Luckily, I had people on my side, and important people too – the police, social services and my solicitors. Even Tricia had agreed to be on standby and come all the way from Norfolk to give evidence against Charlie if she needed to.

Even so, it didn't make me feel confident. Right from the start, I thought he'd get away with it. The police assured me we had a very strong case but I couldn't allow myself to think he'd get sent down.

By now I'd become friendly with Steph, Daniel's ex-girlfriend, and she stayed over with me the night before the court date on Monday for moral support.

The next morning, I got up, put on my best black suit and we got in the car to drive to the Crown Court.

I felt strangely calm that day. It was like everything had been leading up to that moment and now that it was here, I was prepared for what I was about to do.

As we pulled into the car park, I noticed Charlie having a fag outside the court as we got out of the car and for the first time in months, I got a good look at him.

Gone was the confident swagger and smug grin, he was hunched over and drawn, his face pale and set in a mask of grim anticipation.

In his cheap black suit and tie, he looked pathetic and weak, like a man already defeated.

I smiled inwardly then. '*You're going down*,' I thought. '*I've already won one case, I got to keep the kids, and now I'm going to win this.*'

We were shown into the waiting room for the court that morning and at 9 a.m. I was all ready to give my evidence. But they never called me.

As we sat reading magazines, pacing up and down and exchanging nervous conversation, I waited and waited for the time when I would go into court and finally have my say against the man who had stolen my childhood and destroyed my life.

But it never came – every so often someone from the prosecution team would come in and tell us what was going on, updating us on the legal arguments, but still, I wasn't called.

Finally at 3 p.m., my prosecution barrister beckoned me into a small room.

'We need to talk,' she explained as I sat down, confused. 'There have been a few developments but basically you don't need to give evidence.'

Relief swept through my body. I'd been so tense and nervous the whole day and now, I could finally relax, knowing I didn't have to go through with it.

'He's changed his plea to guilty,' she went on. 'We've spent all morning speaking to him and his solicitor and he's agreed to plead guilty on certain charges. He was told that if he pleaded not guilty and was then found guilty by the jury, he'd get a longer sentence. So we've agreed to let him plead to four charges of indecent assault and two charges of indecency with a child.'

So that was it? I didn't get to have my say. I was so angry. I wanted to get in there and tell everybody what he'd done. He'd originally been up on charges of rape, which would have meant a much longer sentence – he'd pleaded not guilty all this time and got me to the point of giving evidence. Then, they'd done a deal and that meant I couldn't go in and tell everyone what he'd done. I started to cry.

'I don't want this,' I said. 'Can't I give my evidence? I want everyone to know exactly what he has done to me and how it's affected me.'

'I'm sorry, Tina,' the barrister said, shaking her head. 'It's done – he's pleaded guilty.'

In the car on the way home, I was angry with Charlie, the prosecution team and everything that had happened. He'd made me get to the point of going to trial before changing his plea and then denied me the chance to tell the world what he'd done!

It felt like he'd managed to shut me up after all. It was his final exertion of control.

*

Charlie, however, pleaded not guilty in the case of the second victim, so the trial went ahead with her evidence and every day the police called me up to let me know how it was progressing.

I didn't know any facts about that case until it came out in court but the similarities to my experiences were striking. It had started when the girl was eight and he'd groomed her by bribing her with sweets and chocolates. Then he'd used aggressive violence to have his way with her, just like he did with me.

On the final day of the trial, I went round to a friend's house, a bundle of nerves.

I kept checking my phone every five minutes and eventually, my friend, who knew about the trial, asked if I'd heard what was going on.

'No, I've not heard a thing,' I replied. 'I'm still waiting for a phone call.'

Just at that second, my phone rang. My heart was racing as I answered. It was Karen, the police officer who'd been with me throughout the case.

'I've got good news for you,' she said. 'He's been found guilty of offences against the second victim.'

My scream was almost deafening. I couldn't believe it and was jumping round the house, ecstatic. Finally, after all these years, Charlie was getting what he deserved! He'd been found guilty of four counts of rape and two of indecent assault in relation to this victim, as well as what he'd pleaded guilty to for me.

*

I could hardly wait for the day of sentencing. After being denied my day in court I wanted to see him sent down once and for all. It finally came two months later and though I was excited, my lawyers prepared me for the fact that he'd get a reduced tariff for the crimes against me because he'd pleaded guilty.

This time, we were due at the old Crown Court but I'd thought we were in the same court as before so Steph and I had to run halfway across town to make it in time.

When we arrived, everyone was already there, waiting to be called in: Charlie's mum Carol and his girlfriend Cheryl on one bench, Pippa on another and then the second victim, the police officer and the lawyers.

Everyone got up slowly but I marched straight through the big double doors first – this was my day. This was the day I'd been waiting for years.

We sat along one big balcony bench – all Charlie's people on one side, and the rest of us on the other. There were benches at the front for the lawyers and at the top was where the judge sat.

In front of us was a great big glass box and after a short while, the prison guard came up through the stairs into the box, followed by Charlie in his black suit, the same black suit he'd had on for the trial. As Charlie looked around the court, he saw me and I looked straight at him. My heart was pounding madly but I didn't blink, didn't even flinch. He looked drained and tired. '*This is what you get,*' I thought, '*for taking away my life.*' I focused all my hate into that stare for as long as it took for him to turn away. In that second, I felt so strong.

Shortly afterwards, the judge came in and after we'd all sat back down again, he started to talk about Charlie's crimes – 'sickening' was what he called him.

I was desperate to hear every single word of the judge's speech but the sound in the court was so muffled, I could barely make out a word.

'What's he saying?' I kept whispering to Karen. Then he started talking about the sentences for all the crimes Charlie had committed. I was adding it all up and I couldn't work out how much it was, then they were reducing it and I didn't know exactly what he was getting.

Finally, Karen turned to me after all the sentences had been read out and smiled: 'He's going down for eleven years!' she whispered.

Eleven years! Fantastic! I was on cloud nine. Now that Charlie was convicted and sentenced, now that the law had put the blame on him for all the years I had suffered at his hands, I could finally start living my life. I would never get back what Charlie had taken from me – my innocence, my trust in people and those sixteen years of living in fear – but I hoped that Charlie would now feel what it was like to lose everything.

Charlie was then taken down the steps towards the cells and as he turned to go down, I saw tears in his eyes. He was crying, but I was laughing. So hard.

*

We walked out of that room and I turned to the second victim. We looked at each other through our tears and then just fell into a massive hug,

'It's over,' she said to me. 'It's finally over.'

The prosecution team took us both into a side room and explained that Charlie would only stay in prison for half his sentence – five and a half years – then he'd be out on parole and if he did anything wrong he'd be sent back inside. He'd be on the sex offenders' register for life and his life was now governed by certain conditions which meant he was never allowed to work with children under sixteen, be in contact with anybody under the age of sixteen or in a relationship with someone who has children under sixteen.

It was disappointing to learn that Charlie would only serve five and a half years in prison; after all I'd spent sixteen long years in the prison he had created for me. But then I found out that he'd only been given three years for the crimes against me, and that really hurt.

He'd been on remand for eighteen months, which meant that by the day of the sentencing, he'd already served his time for me. That was a bitter pill to swallow.

But that day we were driving back in the car listening to the local radio and the news came on – the first item was all about Charlie. I started laughing – now everyone would know he was a 'dangerous paedophile', just as the judge had called him.

We got home in time for the six o'clock news and when the item about Charlie came on the telly, I whipped out my phone and recorded the whole thing.

I'd won. After all these years, and all the pain, I'd finally won!

I sat there that evening thinking back to the day I left him. Two years – that's what he'd said, 'I'll give you two years. Within two years you'll be back here with me.'

Well, two years had passed and he was behind bars.

I was so proud. I'd done it. I was free.

The evening of the sentencing, I went home and told the kids everything that had happened to me. It was important that I could finally tell them face-to-face what their dad had done to me.

It wasn't an easy conversation – Alex thought he should have been put away for longer and Tammy didn't really understand so she was just upset her daddy was in prison – but I told them they could always talk to me if there was anything they wanted to know.

My social worker Pippa had wanted me to wait as *she* wanted to inform the children but I was now ready to take control of my life.

'No, I'm going to tell them,' I said firmly. 'I'm their mother and it's about time they heard the truth from me.'

It was time for me to be left alone to get on with my life.

For a few months after Charlie was sent down I had nightmares every night. I'd dream that he was coming to get me, to pay me back for putting him in jail and I'd wake up in a sweat with flashbacks of all the awful things he'd done to me flooding my brain.

The support centre suggested counselling and that helped me to understand what I was going through and gave me an insight into how the abuse would continue to affect me. It's been a long journey, and there's still a long way to go, but I'm getting stronger every day. I'm a lot more confident than before and seem to cope with everything that's thrown at me. There are still days I feel like it's all too much for me, but something inside keeps telling me: '*Don't give up. You've got to keep fighting.*' And that's what I keep doing. It's difficult. I still look over my shoulder all the time and I'm wary of people but it's going to take a long time to break these habits.

* * *

A few months after the trial we moved out of the area. We were getting abuse shouted at us in the street, we had our windows put through and the tyres on my car were slashed. It was time to make a fresh start and a new life for ourselves where nobody knew us. But even moving away, I began to realise that we would never truly be free.

Charlie took away our chance of ever being a normal family. We can meet new people and the kids can make friends at school, but we'll always have to hide the truth.

How can you explain being abused by your step-father for sixteen years and having his four kids? It's too shocking. Too much to take in and it's frightening. You hear about these things on TV or the radio and you don't imagine them happening to your neighbour across the street or the mum you see at the school gates.

So when I make new friends now I don't come out and tell them what I've been through. And the kids don't say their dad is in prison either. If anyone asks they tell them they don't know their dad. It's a lot easier. Children don't understand and can be cruel.

As for me, I've spent a long time coming to terms with who I am and what I want from life. After so long with Charlie, I feel I deserve to be with someone who will love me and the kids, someone who'll put their arms around me when I'm sad and tell me everything will be okay.

But in the year following the sentencing, while me and the kids settled into our new home, and while I started to find my feet again, I didn't even think about meeting someone. Instead, I threw all my energy into my family.

As time went on, I began to feel something was missing from my life.

There was a guy I'd known for ages through the Internet and even though we'd never actually spoken directly, I'd followed the ups and downs of his life through our mutual friend Diane.

Andy seemed like a lovely person and everything I heard about him made me want to know him better. Eventually we started talking on MSN and he was surprised to find I already knew so much about his life.

We started dating in summer 2009 and the first time we met up I was really nervous.

'*Who'd want me?*' I thought. I felt so tainted by everything I'd been through. But Andy instantly put me at my ease and the more I got to know him, the more I liked him. He knew everything about my past and he didn't seem put off, which showed me that he really was someone of substance.

When we first kissed, it was amazing, so intense I didn't want it to end. Apart from my one-night stand and Kevin he'd been the first person I'd ever kissed properly and it was wonderful, there was so much feeling behind it.

Sex was also an issue for me. But over time I slowly learned that sex is in fact a very natural thing. I even experimented with a vibrator after a friend recommended one to me. I'd never even heard of one before! At the age of twenty-six I had my first orgasm ever. From that point onwards I began to take control of my own sexuality. It wasn't easy at first – there were a lot of conflicting emotions afterwards, and many times after I'd had an orgasm, Charlie's face would pop into my head and I'd be burdened with guilt and shame again.

But over time I managed to wipe the thoughts of him from my mind and just allow myself to let go and enjoy it.

So by the time I met Andy, I felt ready to have a full physical relationship. And he was so kind and gentle. He'd cuddle me and put his arms around me. I'd never had that before. Or just turn round and give me a kiss and tell me he loved me. It felt so right and soon we were planning to move in together.

Now we share a lovely four-bedroom house with a big garden where all the kids can run around and play. And I'm happier than I've ever been in my life.

As for the children, it's still hard with the older two to show them as much love and affection as I'd like – I can't break the habit of a lifetime. I do give them cuddles every now and then but I can't seem to sustain them for very long.

As they get older, I have to deal with a lot of issues which surface from my own childhood. For example, if

Alex comes up and give me a peck on the cheek, I panic. I worry that people will think I'm abusing my children! It sounds crazy, I know, but I'm not like most people – my childhood was warped and I have to struggle to overcome it.

If I'm sitting on the settee and they want to give me a cuddle, I can't. Because that's what Charlie did while he was grooming me. He did so much to destroy my life in so many ways but every day I fight to get over those difficulties.

I'll never be the perfect mother – but I'll always do my best for my kids, I look after them well and give them all the love I can. I always vowed that was what I'd do one day and if you look at how much I've dealt with already, I think it's safe to say I am pretty strong.

Being a stay-at-home mum is all I've known and I'm used to it – this is my life and I love it. At home I'm in total control and I'm happy where I am. I've never been much of a one to go out to pubs and clubs so I don't miss it. My ideal day is taking the kids out for a meal and then going to the park afterwards. It sounds ridiculously simple but then after all the horrors I've faced in my life, the simple things are the ones that make me smile.

Of course I think about how this is going to affect the kids in years to come and I know they're going to struggle. How can it fail to affect them?

I'm especially worried about Alex – he was older and he saw what his dad did and hates him for it. He's got a lot of anger inside him and I just hope that he can come to terms with his past and move on to better things. I'm trying to help him as much as I can.

As for Tammy, she's doing really well. She's had a lot fewer health issues since the transplant, but because of her developmental problems she's a bit slower than all the other kids her age. I hope that one day she'll live a full and independent life but only time will tell whether the chemo has affected her fertility.

After all they've watched me go through, she and Alex are strangely protective of me and it's sweet. As for the younger two, they're just a couple of little monsters, but I love them dearly. I still miss Tom every day. That will never go away.

Charlie told Daniel eventually that I was his sister. I found out one day when I got an upset call from Daniel. It was such a shock to him and has made staying in touch very difficult for us. It's very sad. I do hope he manages to accept his past and move on from it.

Sometimes these days I look back and wonder, '*How did I manage to do that?*' Getting away from Charlie and putting him inside, where did I find the strength? About three months after Charlie had been sentenced, I had an appointment to see my solicitor to go over loads of old papers and in there I found some documents from years back. They were reports from social services and court papers. In them I read how Mum was trying really hard to get me away from Charlie. Right there in front of the solicitor, I broke down. I realised after all this time that she really did love me. She was doing her best but nobody believed her. Charlie managed to twist everyone round to his way of thinking. It was then I realised I hadn't just gone through the trial for myself and my kids, I had helped put Charlie away for her too. The woman who had given me life but, because of her illness, had never learned how to show me love.

All my life I dreamed of having someone to love me, and that's all it was, just a dream, until the day it finally came true. After all I went through; all the pain, the hurt and the abuse, I eventually won. I was free. For so long people had told me to leave, to get out of the situation I was in with but it's hard when there is no one to turn to and nowhere to go. Fear takes over and you become imprisoned in a cell made not of bars and concrete but of threats and abuse and mind games.

But no matter how hard things are, no matter how scared you feel, it can be done; you can break free and change your life. I am living proof of that. No one should have to suffer like I did. I felt weak and ashamed of what he did to me, I was scared and I didn't want to go on any more. Yet I found the strength to fight back and now, after sixteen years, I've finally found happiness. Finally, my dream has come true.

I'll never forget what I went through but you learn to live one day at a time. No matter how alone you feel there is always someone there to help, no matter how hard things are. Hope lives on.

Acknowledgements

I would like to thank:

Andy, for being my rock, making my dreams come true and for being there for me. I love you so much.

My wonderful children – Mummy loves you always.

Tricia, without you I wouldn't be here today. You helped me in so many ways and I can't thank you enough for everything you did for me.

Marie – thank you for being a true friend.

Katy Weitz for all you have done for me and for helping me to tell my story.

And finally, a big thank you to all the people that know me and have helped me in the past three years – family, friends and support workers.

About the Author

Since seeing the man who abused her as child be sent to jail, Tina Davis has focused on rebuilding her life. She now has five children all together and lives in the north-east of England where she has created a happy home for herself and her cherished family. She urges anybody suffering domestic or sexual violence to contact Women's Aid on **0800 2000247** or visit www.womensaid.org.uk.